Ethnic Minorities in the Inner City:

The Ethnic Dimension in Urban Deprivation in England

Crispin Cross

Published by

Commission for Racial Equality
Elliot House
10-12 Allington Street
Lonson, SW1E 5EH

© Commission for Racial Equality

First edition
August 1978

ISBN 0 902355 77 5 ✓

010 8619

Printed by Interlink Longraph Ltd, London.

*"It may be that blacks are in the same boat
as poor whites; but we are on different decks"*

Tony Ottey

Short Note on the Author

Crispin Cross holds the BSc (soc) Hons, the MSc (econ) and the PhD degrees from the London School of Economics, University of London. He has taught at the Polytechnic of Central London, the London School of Economics and at the North East London Polytechnic where he was also responsible for coordinating postgraduate supervision and research within the Faculty of Human Sciences. He was Principal Research Officer at the Community Relations Commission and is presently Head of the Research Department at the Commission for Racial Equality in London. Among his many publications are *Interviewing and Communication in Social Work*, London: Routledge & Kegan Paul, 1974.

Contents

Appendices

List of Tables

Acknowledgements

We were indebted to Political and Economic Planning and to David Smith in particular for giving us access to the manuscript of their "National Survey of Racial Minorities" and for permitting us to draw from it in connection with Housing. This survey was subsequently published under the title **The Facts of Racial Disadvantage.** However, reference to this work in this volume is made to the manuscript material.

We are also grateful to many individuals for their assistance with this study. It is undoubtedly invidious to mention names, nevertheless Sue Wallis assisted with the administration of the project; Dr. Kenneth Pryce and Cathy Carmichael assisted with the interviews in various parts of the country. Mr. Peter Tucker, Dr. Muhammad Anwar, Philip Nanton, Jenny Griffin and Simon Williams acted as 'devil's advocates' and read previous drafts of the manuscript of this study either in parts or as a whole. But undoubtedly, the project could not have been undertaken without the generous help and co-operation of the Chief Executives, Heads of Departments and other senior officers of the local authorities in the various project areas and without the co-operation of social workers, teachers, youth workers, home help organisers, community centre wardens, day nursery matrons, playgroup leaders and many lay persons, both white and from ethnic minority communities, in these areas who gave us some of their time and participated in the interviews. Needless to say, none of them is responsible for the ideas advanced in this volume.

Preface

The aim of the investigation reported in this volume was to examine the social needs of ethnic minority residents of urban areas, determine the extent to which they are similar to or are different from those of their indigenous counterparts in these areas and explore the implications of these similarities and differences for the regeneration of the quality of life in the inner city. In the course of carrying out this aim, this volume describes the social disadvantages which ethnic minority communities experience in Housing, Education, the Social Services, Youth and Community facilities and their concentration among the deprived/disadvantaged population. It also describes the existence of special patterns of multiple disadvantages which affects them as well as the existence of special needs which derive partly from their newness to this society and partly from their cultural backgrouns.

This investigation was undertaken in eight urban areas in various regions throughout the country and involved interviews with three groups of people as follows;

(a) 'decision-makers' (i.e. local councillors and Directors of local authority departments) in the project areas who are responsible for matters pertaining to Housing, Social Services, Education, Youth and Community facilities;

(b) 'professional practitioners' in these areas (e.g. day nursery matrons, home help organisers, social workers, teachers, wardens of community centres, youth workers — both club based and detached) and

(c) 'lay persons' drawn from ethnic minority communities as well as from the indigenous population in the eight project areas in which the research investigation was undertaken.

A total of 1,684 people were interviewed altogether, of whom 86 were 'decision-makers' within local authorities, 195 were 'professional practitioners', and 1,403 were 'laymen' drawn from ethnic minorities and the indigenous population.

From the outset, it was decided to focus on those services which local authorities provide to meet the social needs of their residents for a number of reasons. First, local authorities are statutory bodies for administering the widest range of services within their boundaries and are therefore in a position to ensure that these services reach those who need them most across the areas

10

of Housing, Education, Social Services, Youth and Community facilities. Second, in providing these services for their residents, local authorities act as a mechanism for implementing central government policies within these 'main programme' services even though these authorities constitute a different tier of administration from that of the central government and the civil service. Third, such central government programmes as have been directed at dealing with some of the problems resulting from urban deprivation have been channelled through local authorities e.g. funds under the Urban Aid Programme and under Section 11 of the Local Government (Grants and Needs) Act, 1966. Further, programmes for regenerating the inner city are therefore likely to be either channelled directly through these authorities or may require a high degree of participation by them. For all these reasons, local authorities remain the statutory mechanisms for administering and providing services to meet the social needs of residents in their areas.

However, employment is not a statutory responsibility of local authorities but is the concern of the private sector primarily, except in so far as:

(a)   local authorities are often the largest employers of labour within their areas and are thus in a position to provide a lead for the private sector to follow in their employment practices and,

(b)   are now obliged under Section 71 of the Race Relations Act, 1976 to promote equality of opportunity in the administration of those services for which they have statutory responsibilities as well as in their employment practices.

It was therefore felt, at the design stage, that this investigation was best carried out with a strong emphasis on those services which local authorities provide to meet the needs of their residents. This emphasis also had the advantage of simplifying the design considerations which had to be taken into account since it eliminated the role of the private sector altogether.

However, we provide a review of the employment circumstances of ethnic minority workers in the urban areas to which they were attracted when they migrated into the country in order to provide a rounded presentation of the circumstances of life in these areas (and unemployment constitutes an important component of urban deprivation) and in order to demonstrate the extent to which their needs in the sphere of employment differ from those of their indigenous counterparts.

Our findings point to the need for;

(a)   priority to be given to ethnic minorities in social policies in the light of their greater need in general and in policies directed at alleviating some of the consequences of multiple deprivation in particular;

(b)   modifications or adaptations in the ways in which social policies generally and specific programmes to combat multiple deprivation are *presented* to ethnic minority residents; and

11

(c) special programmes need to be developed for ethnic minority groups to meet those of their needs which are particular to them and do not affect the indigenous population (e.g. second language tuition facilities).

We also go on to discuss the need for financial arrangements which could facilitate these approaches and, at the same time, enable local authorities to review their priorities, modify the way they present and 'deliver' their services as well as develop special services to meet those needs which are particular to these groups. These arrangements should also include assistance to these authorities to enable them to fund self-help activities by the ethnic minority communities themselves which should enable them to meet part of their needs which are peculiar to their cultural backgrounds.

A brief discussion of the major lines of policy to which these conclusions point was presented in a booklet *Urban Deprivation, Racial Inequality and Social Policy* (London: HMSO) by the former Community Relations Commission in 1977 as well as in two articles by the author in *New Community* and the *Human Rights Review*[1] respectively. However, this volume reports the details of the methodology and results of the investigation in full in the context of the main programme areas within which it was conducted so that those who work within these programme areas can determine how these results relate to the exercise of their specialisms in their own areas.

Its publication is also timely since considerable discussion has gone on and will continue on the general problem of the need to regenerate the inner city, the various ways in which this can be done, the agencies which can contribute towards such a regeneration and, indeed, the extent to which these agencies require special legal powers to enable them to do so — all of these being issues which were reflected in the White Paper on Inner Cities published in June, 1977 as well as in the Inner Urban Areas Act, 1977. In this regard, the fact that ethnic minorities from the New Commonwealth tend to live in inner city areas which this volume underlines, should stimulate an awareness of the need for an ethnic minority dimension in all programmes which are aimed at regenerating the inner city. To this extent, the general reader as well as the specialist will find much in this volume to stimulate an awareness of the range and extent of the problem of urban deprivation on the one hand as well as the need for an ethnic minority dimension in inner city policies in general and in the delivery of social resources by local authorities on the other.

In preparing this volume, we were conscious of the possibility that such terms as 'black people', 'coloured people', 'New Commonwealth born persons', 'immigrants'[2], 'whites', 'indigenous people' and 'ethnic minorities' may be misleading to some people and offensive to others. However, to have adopted a uniform and possibly less objectionable common term (even if one could be found) would have minimised the richness of the responses which we obtained from the 1,684 respondents who participated in the interviews and who, without exception, used one or a combination of the terms mentioned above synonymously to refer to Asians, West Indians, Africans and Cypriots on the one hand and white British people on the other.

But apart from using these different terms to refer to the ethnic minority and indigenous groups who participated in the study, we have also followed the path of simplicity in referring to all senior officials in local authorities who are in a position to determine and influence policy as 'decision-makers' irrespective of whether they were Directors of Housing, Housing Managers, Directors of Social Services etc. or the elected Councillors with special responsibilities for any of the main programmes — Education, Housing, Youth, Social Services etc. Similarly, we have referred to all those officers who were involved with the daily administration of these various main programme areas when the study was carried out, be they teachers, social workers, youth workers etc, as 'professional practitioners'. Similarly, we have referred to the various groups of interviewees as 'laymen' irrespective of whether they were West Indians, Pakistanis, Bangladeshis, East African Asians, Greek or Turkish Cypriots except where their countries of origin are relevant to the analysis under discussion. It would clearly have been impossible to maintain simplicity and ease of description, if we had attempted to do otherwise.

Chapter One: Introduction

Urban Deprivation and Ethnic Minorities in England
It is often assumed that urban deprivation became an issue of public concern and a focus of government policy only during the decade of the sixties and that its causes, and not only its consequences, are products of the twentieth century. On the contrary, the causes of urban deprivation go back to the circumstances surrounding the emergence of Great Britain as an industrial power during the Industrial Revolution and the heightened degree of urbanization which followed in its wake. Government concern with its effects on the lives of people who live in urban areas is not as recent as it is often assumed to be and goes back to the early part of this century when it became apparent that central and local government action was necessary to stem the continuing decay of inner city areas and to encourage 'dispersal' of industry to the new and expanding towns and suburbs. The destruction of the inner areas of many cities during the Second World War was therefore followed not only by a concern to reconstruct them but also to improve the quality of life of those people who live in these areas at the same time.

This concern was given added impetus by a recognition that the immigration of New Commonwealth persons into the connurbations in search of employment was likely to increase the strain which the social services and other local government services in these areas would experience, in having to contend not only with the needs of indigenous people who live in these areas and who may themselves have migrated to them in search of better employment opportunities but also with the needs of different groups of immigrants with cultural backgrounds and languages which are different from those of the host population. This recognition was important not only in providing an added emphasis to central government's concern with urban deprivation but was also crucial in ensuring that one central government department took overall responsibility for co-ordinating policies which are aimed at ameliorating some of the consequences, if not all, of urban deprivation.

The Notion of Urban Deprivation
However, there is no precise and generally agreed definition of the term 'urban deprivation' in spite of the widespread and justifiable attention which it

commands. It is generally accepted that 'urban deprivation' is a corporate term which embraces a number of specific aspects of life in an inner city area ranging from people's inability to influence the processes of decision-making in local areas to the existence of people who are socially disadvantaged in terms of their low income, low socio-economic status, and low utilisation of various locally administered facilities and so on.

In this regard an interesting investigation was undertaken for the Home Office Deprivation Unit[1] into the meaning of the term 'urban deprivation' among senior local government officials who are responsible for administering various services. This investigation underscored the absence of a generally agreed meaning for the concept. It showed that there was a clear tendency for officials to attribute a meaning to the concept which is closely related to the services for which they are responsible. Thus, officials who were concerned with Housing matters tended to define urban deprivation in terms of the physical characteristics of the area in which they work, the extent of overcrowding and the number of dwellings which are in multi-occupation and so on. Those who worked in the Social Services thought of urban deprivation in terms of the prevalence of social problems among various categories of the population in the areas for which they are responsible. Inevitably, the prevalence of 'problem families' featured in their conception of an area of urban deprivation.

It should perhaps not be surprising that the meaning attributed to the term 'urban deprivation' by these officials should be closely related to their professional specialisms. But what this investigation did emphasise is the need for close integration of these various specialisms so as to ensure that urban deprivation — being the generic entity that it is — can receive the co-ordinated impact of these services on a local level and, eventually, on a national level. To the extent that the term 'urban deprivation' is given meaning in terms of particular specialisms, to the same extent would co-ordination of local services in areas of urban deprivation require a particular managerial approach. It was with a view to finding out how such managerial co-ordination can be effected that the Inner Areas Studies were launched under the auspices of the Department of the Environment.

The problem of definition apart, however, there are a number of *core* ideas which are brought into sharp relief by the use of the term 'urban deprivation'. These ideas account, to a large extent, for the justifiable degree of public concern which the concept tends to arouse.

First, an area of urban deprivation can be so described to the extent that it incorporates physical characteristics which impair the quality of life of those who live in it and cannot escape from it. These physical characteristics include, *inter alia* a general absence of play areas for children, a lack of other recreational facilities for public use, an unplanned co-existence of factories and homes, a relatively large number of old and dilapidated homes which are in multi-occupation and lack basic amenities, and unemployment. In effect, the environmental characteristics of such an area tend to impair the quality of life of those who live in it and are unable to escape from it. They tend, in this physical sense, to be deprived compared to those who are able to live outside it.

Second, an area of urban deprivation is often marked by a relatively low provision of services and facilities to people who need them most by virtue of their economic poverty. Such poverty often reflects the existence of pockets of unemployment within the inner city or a general lack of the appropriate qualifications which are required for such jobs as are to be found in an urban environment. The low provision of services and facilities often reflects the pressure of demand over the supply of resources, for the inner city incorporates socially disadvantaged groups either because industries move away from the inner city areas leaving pockets of unemployment behind or because the psychological circumstances of particular groups of people pre-dispose them towards becoming casualties of the welfare state e.g. the homeless, the unemployed school-leaver, the single parent family, the elderly etc. The range of people who are socially disadvantaged in areas of urban deprivation is often so wide that they pose complex administrative problems to those who are responsible for administering such facilities.

This sets up a vicious circle in which administrative and financial resources are often in short supply to meet the ever-growing problems of the socially disadvantaged which are generated in the inner city and which in turn require additional administrative and financial resources.[2]

Third, an area of urban deprivation incorporates socially disadvantaged groups of persons partly because such persons are attracted to it in their search for better living and other opportunities and partly because such an environment incorporates groups of people who are the victims of the so-called 'cycle of deprivation' (or transmitted deprivation).

Sir Keith Joseph once called attention to the possibility of the existence of cyclical factors in the transmission of deprivation from one generation to another in a speech he made in 1972 to the Pre-School Playgroups Association,[3] in which he said "Perhaps there is at work here a process, apparent in many situations but imperfectly understood, by which problems reproduce themselves from generation to generation. If I refer to this as a 'cycle of deprivation' I do not want to be misunderstood. On the one hand the use of such a term may suggest rather more certainty about the phenomenon I am trying to describe than the state of our understanding warrants; on the other hand, I may be accused of talking about the blindingly obvious"[4] The rest of the Secretary of State's speech was received with critical acclaim but his description of the 'cycle of deprivation' as a generator of some aspects of the social problems which emerge in an urban environment was not challenged. In this regard, social workers, teachers and policemen have highlighted situations in which children of a family with social problems, be it delinquency and crime, large families or low income, go on to 'repeat' the same patterns of problems during their own adulthood. Some research has been commissioned by the Social Science Research Council and the Department of Health & Social Security which should throw some light on how cyclical factors of deprivation operate from one generation to another and how that cycle can be broken.[5] Such research should also illuminate the processes by which areas of urban deprivation generate at least some categories of socially disadvantaged people.

There is one school of thought which suggests that socially disadvantaged groups of people tend to be generated in other geographical areas and are merely attracted to the urban environment because of the facilities and services which it offers. It would be impossible to deny that a certain amount of drift has contributed to some of the problems which have emerged in urban areas e.g. overcrowding, multi-occupation of dwellings, highly mobile populations of tenants in privately rented accommodation, delinquency and crime. To be sure, rural-urban migration has been a permanent feature not only of Britain ever since the Industrial Revolution but of every industrial country as well. Such migration increased the heterogeneity of the population in urban areas considerably even before immigrants from the New Commonwealth arrived in these areas during the decade of the sixties.

Nevertheless, not all of the problems which have been found in areas of urban deprivation can be attributed to the effect of 'drift' migration. Urban areas do, in fact, produce various categories of socially disadvantaged people partly because of the 'cycle of deprivation' and partly because of a combination of reasons connected with poor housing, unemployment, low income, poverty and so on. We shall deal with some of these in greater detail in the later chapters of this volume.

However, research into the causes of urban deprivation can only be useful in illuminating some of the circumstances surrounding the decay of inner city areas; it cannot provide practical solutions in the short run. Indeed, it is doubtful whether such research can do more than demonstrate the relative contributions of the 'drift' theory and the 'cycle of deprivation' theory to the emergence of the problems that characterise such areas or whether such a demonstration would not in the main be largely irrelevant to the practical need to tackle some, if not all, of the social problems which have been associated with urban deprivation in the past. Such research studies will undoubtedly contribute towards a clarification of the philosophical rationale of policies which are aimed at combating urban deprivation in the long run. Of more practical relevance in the short-term however, is the impact of the initiatives which central and local government have taken towards areas of urban deprivation.

Clearly, then, the concept of urban deprivation is not a unitary one but incorporates a number of characteristics of inner city areas. These characteristics have been isolated here but do not stand in isolation from each other in reality. Bad and inadequate housing is not confined to urban areas but can be found in rural areas as well. Equally, there are socially disadvantaged groups of people in rural areas as well as in urban areas. Similarly, many residents in rural areas do not profit from or take advantage of local authority services and are, in this respect at least, not very different from residents in urban areas. In this sense, deprivation is not an urban phenomenon in itself but is relative to the advantages which other people enjoy irrespective of the geographical area in which they live.[6]

What is distinctive about urban deprivation is that these three core ideas tend to be found more often together in urban areas and involve relatively larger numbers of people than in rural areas. Urban deprivation has therefore become the focus of government policies largely because of the statistical concentration of social problems in urban areas rather than out of a lack of concern with deprived people in rural areas.

Since this is so, a concern with urban deprivation cannot be confined to the existence of persons who are 'deprived' in the sense that they are unable to cope with the standards which are expected of them either in relation to the social services or in relation to housing. It cannot, of course, be denied that areas of urban deprivation are likely to contain larger proportions of people who are 'deprived' in this pathological sense of the term; rather, a concern with urban deprivation which is restricted to this pathological group of persons is likely to underplay other and wider problems concerning the availability of resources (both financial and administrative) for social facilities and services, the importance of adequate management co-ordination of the various services which are provided on a local level and also underplay the importance of strategic planning in urban areas in particular.

We stress this point not only because of the general difficulty of defining urban deprivation in a simple way to which we referred earlier but also because at least one central government initiative which was launched on the 'pathological' conception of urban deprivation had to be revised in the light of the field experience of those who were responsible for operationalising it throughout the country. These fieldworkers called for a greater stress on the structural conditions pertaining to areas of urban deprivation rather than on the social pathology of groups of people who live within these areas.

We designed the project reported in this volume on the basis of the generic conception of urban deprivation outlined above rather than on the pathological conception. We did this in order to capture and reflect situations in which either the necessary social and other facilities for people living in urban areas are not available for various reasons — administrative as well as financial — or, where they are available, are not being utilised for any of a number of reasons. We were also anxious to capture and examine situations in which the presence of New Commonwealth immigrants had *not* made an impact on either the style of presentation or, indeed on the content of various services and facilities which are provided on a local level.

In this connection, we have had to be circumspect about the often-expressed assumption that New Commonwealth immigrants in urban areas are the socially disadvantaged and vice versa largely because it over-simplifies the true position and because it gives equal weight to the factors which identify both the socially disadvantaged and New Commonwealth immigrants. We have found, in this investigation, that there are some factors which are somewhat specific to these immigrants — racial discrimination in general and especially from employers, their inability to use the English language as a first language in the case of some members of some minority groups and the fact that their religious and cultural backgrounds are different from those of the host population.

Indeed, an investigation into poverty in Camden which was undertaken by the Institute of Community Studies demonstrated that New Commonwealth immigrants do not necessarily constitute part of the population of that area who live below the poverty line, thus reinforcing the point made above.[7] It demonstrated that those who live below the poverty line are one-parent families, elderly couples and heads of households across both indigenous and ethnic minority groups.

It would clearly be foolish to generalise from this finding in the Camden area either to the effect that there are no immigrants living in poverty in urban areas or to other areas in the country particularly as the ethnic minority groups in the Camden area are not randomly distributed throughout the rest of the country. Nevertheless, this finding does provide some justification for not assuming that immigrants are necessarily disadvantaged or, where they are disadvantaged, that they are disadvantaged for the same sets of reasons as apply to the population at large. Our investigation has shown that there are other criteria such as racial discrimination, language difficulties, cultural and religious issues, unfamiliarity with British institutions etc. which contribute towards social disadvantage among immigrants and which do not necessarily apply to the indigenous population but which require some attention from policymakers.

Since the project reported in this volume was not based on the 'pathological' conception of urban deprivation while at least one central government initiative was based on it, it is as well to describe the varius central and local government initiatives which have been launched over the past few years and which constituted the backcloth against which our investigation was undertaken.

Central Government Initiatives on Urban Deprivation up to 1977
The National Community Development Project was conceived in the late sixties and launched in 1969. It was a major experiment in action-research in Britain which was to run for an experimental period of five years in twelve project areas with an average population size of 15,000 people. It was aimed at (a) improving the quality of individual and community life in areas with a high level of social need through programmes of social action which draw on local resources; (b) increasing the range of social and economic opportunities for people living in the communities in the project areas; (c) creating an increased capacity for individuals and communities to take advantage of opportunities which exist in local areas and (d) assisting individuals and communities in the project areas to exercise self-determination in their own lives.[8]

Most of the twelve project areas were in inner city areas and several incorporated large tracts with public housing and run-down private accommodation. The twelve project areas selected were Paisley (near Glasgow), Newcastle and North Shields in Northumberland, Cleator Moor, Oldham, Liverpool, Batley, Birmingham, Coventry, Glyncorrwg in Wales, Newham and Southwark in London.

Within each area, an action team was set up to establish contact with the various communities and with local resource agencies — voluntary bodies, local authorities — as well as a research team. The cost of the programme was met by the central government through funds made available under a special Urban Aid Programme budget and administered by the Community Programmes Department of the Home Office.

Several reports from the various project areas stressed the difficulty of working with a conception of urban deprivation which directs attention to individual pathologies and called for a shift towards a conception of urban deprivation which stresses the structural conditions which obtain within these areas — unemployment, declining industries within the inner city and the inability of many residents in project areas to move out as industries decline. The initial conception of urban deprivation in the National Development Project in 1969 was that the problem of deprivation has its origins in the 'deprived' characteristics of local populations and that these could be dealt with by better field/action co-ordination of the personal social services in the project areas together with improved capacities for self-help from within the community. The reports all stressed that the sources of the problem of urban deprivation are to be found in the structural characteristics of these areas and that only massive changes in these characteristics are likely to work.[9]

Accordingly, the key issues which the project reports identified are employment (as a result of industrial change and re-deployment of the labour force), social income and housing. Certainly, in the two project areas which contain sizeable proportions of ethnic minority communities — Saltley (Birmingham) and Batley — the issue of housing and the fairness of existing allocation procedures as well as matters relating to the social income such as entitlement to improvement grants, mortgages etc. baulked large, quite apart from particular disadvantages which are closely related to the background of those immigrant groups who live in those areas e.g. language, culture and religion.

A second central government initiative was the so-called "Six Towns Studies" which was launched in 1972 by the Department of the Environment and was focused primarily on the physical conception of urban deprivation. All six studies were launched with the aim of developing a total approach to the improvement of the environment in the inner city through better area management co-ordination. These studies consisted of three studies undertaken in Oldham, Rotherham and Sunderland, designed to assist local authorities develop a broad approach to the identification of problems in these towns by looking at them as wholes. These three are sometimes referred to separately as the "Urban Guidelines Studies". They were completed in 1973 and the reports were published by HMSO under the title "Making Towns Better". The other three, sometimes referred to separately as the "Inner Area Studies" were completed in 1977/78. They were action-research studies which were aimed at examining particular inner city areas of Birmingham, Lambeth and Liverpool with a view to determining how resources and techniques available within these areas could be best deployed from the point of view of the people who live in these areas. The racial composition of the population in these towns and its implications were not central to these studies.

The reports of the 'Inner Area Studies'[10] reflect not only an awareness of the relationship between the issues that emerge on a high level in these areas (the macro-level) and the individual problems of residents (access to locally provided services) but also an awareness of the extent to which the presence of New Commonwealth immigrants impinge more directly on some issues (e.g. housing) than on others. In this way, they reflect an awareness of the possibility that there are unique issues pertaining to immigrants in these areas which cannot be generalised to other residents. In general, these studies explored not only the major structural problems that emerge in inner city areas (and, indeed, the tendency for these areas to expand over time) such as housing stress and multi-occupation in particular, unemployment among the skilled and the unskilled as against a general expansion of the commercial sector on the one hand and the individual dispositions of residents (such as their awareness and use of personal social services, their desire to move out to the more salubrious suburbs even while being unable to marshal the resources needed to do so) on the other. The consultants in the Lambeth study in this connection, referred to the inner city areas as 'traps' to highlight the extent to which various categories of people are unable to move out even though they are willing to do so.[11]

A third central government initiative but one which was launched earlier than the two discussed above is the Urban Aid Programme. Its origins reach back to political decisions taken in 1965 which were concerned with the need for improving both race relations and immigration control amidst considerable political controversy.[12] It is a programme of local authority expenditure supported by 75% grants from central government and was launched by the Local Government Grants (Social Need) Act of 1969. Grants are made out of this programme in response to periodic circulars from the designated department of government which is also responsible for co-ordinating the programme throughout the country. Over 4,000 projects ranging from nursery school provision, housing aid centres, adventure playgrounds to community centres in urban areas have been financed out of this programme.

Extensive criticisms have been expressed about the process by which grants are allocated, the priority ratings which projects command in local areas as against the priority ratings which the designated government department allocates to projects which it finances; they have also dealt with the general difficulty which many local authorities experience in providing their 25% contributions from their own resources. Indeed, many of the senior officials who were interviewed in connection with this project were extremely critical of these and other aspects of the Urban Aid Programme.

Nevertheless, the Urban Aid Programme is unique insofar as it is concerned with the practical matter of providing additional resources for local authorities in urban areas which contain areas of social need, defined in a general way, rather than a research programme which looks to the future even though the sums that are allocated can be criticised as being 'penny packs' in urban situations where massive injections would have been preferred by many local authorities. It is also unique since it incorporates a policy of 'positive discrimination' in favour of areas which have many of the core problems that characterise areas of urban deprivation even though it is this policy of discrimination against those authorities which do not have such problems (or cannot demonstrate that they have them) which was one of the earliest sources of political controversy. This policy of discrimination has made it possible for local authorities to make some provision for particular categories of people within their areas who have special needs vis a vis others.

For example, it has been possible to provide for the needs of some categories of immigrants by virtue of the fact that they require more child-care facilities (especially nurseries) than other sections of the population in some areas of urban deprivation simply by providing more of these services. We have highlighted the extent to which the children of some categories of immigrants tend to be more at risk (statistically) than other people who live in areas of urban deprivation in an earlier publication.[13]

However, and despite this, there are many problems attendant on the Urban Aid Programme which only a full-scale evaluation would demonstrate. Such an evaluation has been commissioned by the Home Office.[14]

Other central and local government initiatives on urban deprivation can be mentioned *en passant* though there is no room in this report for an extensive evaluation of their impact to date.

One of the most significant initiatives is the series of studies which were undertaken under the Educational Priority Area Projects under the direction of Dr. A. H. Halsey, and funded by the Department of Education and Science. The reports of these projects were published between 1972 and 1975,[15] and resulted in a policy of extra payments to teachers in schools in urban areas which qualify as EPA schools; they have also resulted in the setting up of special centres within the Department of Education and Science to deal with the needs of the educationally disadvantaged in schools.[16]

Another initiative was undertaken by the Home Office who set up a special Home Office Urban Deprivation Unit to prepare Comprehensive Community Programmes for areas of urban deprivation. These programmes were aimed at identifying a number of the most deprived areas on the basis of an analysis of their social and physical characteristics and providing a mechanism for continuous review in terms of employment, housing, education, health, social services, physical environment and other needs. On the basis of these studies, specific proposals would be submitted to central government for approval, financial assistance and action.[17] A similar initiative was planned by the Greater London Council.[18]

All these initiatives underscore the fact that urban deprivation is a matter of widespread and justifiable concern even though they did not all reflect a commonly agreed and simple definition of the notion. They all reflected not only a concern with the physical characteristics of urban areas but also with the extent to which particular categories of people are able to benefit from such facilities as are available or are unable to do so owing to their own 'deprived' condition. In this sense, and irrespective of the conception of urban deprivation with which they may have been launched, they also reflected a concern with the extent to which these core characteristics interpenetrate and reinforce each other in various ways which are not yet clearly understood. Understandably, therefore, they were all aimed at practical and specific action in urban areas either in the short term in the case of the Urban Programme or in the long term in the case of those which involved action/research.

Race Relations in the Inner City: Towards a Strategy

In its concern with practical action in areas of urban deprivation, the central government has embraced a policy of strong anti-discrimination legislation combined with a policy of general provision for all those who live in such areas irrespective of their racial, cultural and religious backgrounds on the presumption that (a) a policy *of general* provision would benefit members of ethnic minority groups as well as members of the indigenous population *and* (b) it would also contribute towards equality of treatment of all groups in urban areas thus conforming with the general political ideals of successive governments.

This general approach can be illustrated by several government publications. For example, the White Paper on Racial discrimination stated that:

"Beyond the problems of cultural alien-ness, there are the problems of low status, of material and environmental deprivation which coloured immigrants and, increasingly, their children experience. To the extent that they share all or some of these problems with other groups in society, a general attack on deprivation will be relevant to their problems."[19]

In this way, it clearly endorsed a policy of general provision for those who live in areas of urban deprivation rather than particular and specific provision for racial minorities. The Secretary of State for the Environment endorsed this policy in *Race Relations and Housing* when he stated that:

"While immigrants and their families living in inner urban areas share the disadvantages of those areas with the very many others living there, they may have added difficulties of racial discrimination, of gaining access to information, of understanding housing law, procedures and practice."[20]

He thus acknowledged various respects in which the situation of immigrants might differ from those of indigenous people living in these areas but presumed that they are somewhat peripheral to the main problems of urban deprivation which they share with indigenous communities and therefore endorsed a policy of providing housing facilities for all those who live in areas of urban deprivation. Another White Paper, published earlier, stressed precisely the same approach in relation to Education when it stated that:

"Where immigrants and their children live in the older urban and industrial areas, the majority of their children are likely to share with the indigenous children of those areas the educational disadvantages associated with an impoverished environment. The Government believes that immigrant pupils will accordingly benefit increasingly from special help given to *all* those suffering from educational disadvantages."[21]

It went on to acknowledge the possibility that these children may have needs which are specifically related to their alien-ness or their immigrant backgrounds which would have to be taken into account.

But its overall emphasis was on the policy of general provision for all children living in areas of urban deprivation. The Report of the Central Policy Review Staff on 'A Joint Framework for Social Policies' similarly stressed a policy of general provision in the context of urban deprivation policies when it stated that:

"We are here (in the context of urban deprivation policies) concerned with poverty in a wider sense: the condition of people whose command over resources generally — income, educational and occupational skills, environment at home or at work, material possessions falls very seriously short of the average in the community. A 'poverty strategy' must be consistent with social policy towards the community as a whole."[22]

Further illustrations of the twin bases of government policy can be drawn from the speeches delivered in the House of Commons during the Second Reading of the Race Relations Bill on Thursday, 4th March, 1976:

"Members of Britain's racial minorities are entitled to full and equal treatment regardless of their colour, race or national origins ... Although effective legislation against racial discrimination is a necessary condition of equal opportunity and good race relations, it is not in itself a sufficient or complete condition ... A wide range of administrative and voluntary measures is needed in order to give practical effect to the objectives of the law. These measures are needed not only to combat discrimination and encourage equal opportunity but also to tackle what has come to be known as racial disadvantage."

Mr. Roy Jenkins (Home Secretary)

"In real life the lot of the poor coloured immigrant is beset by two quite separate hazards. One is unfair discrimination, based upon prejudice. Against that we can make, have made and should make laws. However, the other hazard, which is much more intractable and, in my submission, much more persuasive, is inescapable discrimination based on disadvantage. The discriminations interact upon each other and form an amalgam, but both can be tackled by Government action."

Mr. Michael Allison (Conservative MP)

"Anti-discrimintion laws in themselves are not enough. Action must be taken to combat the disadvantage experienced by many people in minority communities — real disadvantage, not merely discrimination. The new body (The Commission for Racial Equality) needs resources to combat this."

Mr. A. J. Beith (Liberal MP)

These illustrations clearly underscore the policy of general provision for urban deprivation areas which is implicit in the initiatives which have been taken by central and local government to which we referred earlier.

There is no doubt that ethnic minorities share some disadvantages with their indigenous counterparts in areas of urban deprivation. But they also have various needs which are peculiar to them. Can these needs be met by a policy of general provision? To what extent are these needs reflected in areas of urban deprivation? To what extent do they form part of the geography of urban deprivation in the country? As our orientation towards these questions and as our point of departure for the investigation which is reported in this volume, we examined the geographical spread of urban deprivation and its relationship to the geography of immigrant residence over the past few years.

The Geography of Urban Despair: Statistical Indicators

Discussions about urban deprivation before 1971 reflected the justifiable concern which many people feel towards the problems of those who live in areas of deprivation but was not based on hard statistical data. The 1971 Census ward data library made it possible to examine various statistical aspects of the problem throughout the country since it is based on enumeration districts and is focused on the level of individual enumeration. This makes it possible to collect somewhat comparable figures for the conurbations throughout the country. There are undoubtedly various defects in the Census which have to be weighed against this. First, there is the well-known problem of the under-enumeration of various categories of people especially, in the context of our project, members of ethnic minorities. Second, the Census dealt with some but not all of the indices which are relevant to assessing the quality of life which people enjoy in areas of urban deprivation. For example, it dealt with housing, basic amenities, types of tenure and unemployment (those who seek work or are sick). It did not deal with total earnings, age or condition of housing, security of tenure especially for those who live in privately rented accommodation, underemployment etc. Nevertheless, in spite of these limitations, the ward data library makes it possible to discover, statistically at least, some of the characteristics of urban deprivation as it affects the country as a whole on roughly comparable bases.

A series of investigations of these data by the Department of the Environment[23] showed that there tends to be a relatively high correlation between various indices of urban deprivation in the conurbations. It shows that:
(a) the worst enumeration districts in terms of every indicator of urban deprivation tend to be found in Scotland as against England and Wales except on one index — shared dwellings — in connection with which the situation is worse in England;
(b) the 5% worst areas in terms of having to share hot water facilities are

Clydeside, the ILEA boroughs in London, Merseyside and West Midlands conurbations in that order;

(c) the 5% worst conurbations in terms of sharing or lacking a back are Clydeside, the ILEA boroughs, Merseyside and Tyneside;

(d) the 5% worst conurbations in terms of lacking an inside WC are Tyneside, Merseyside, S.E. Lancashire, Clydeside and W. Midlands;

(e) the 5% worst conurbations in terms of overcrowding (measured on the statutory criterion of there being more than 1.5 persons per room) are Clydeside, the ILEA boroughs, the W. Midlands and W. Yorkshire;

(f) the 5% worst conurbations in terms of lacking all the basic amenities are Clydeside, the ILEA boroughs, Tyneside and Merseyside;

(g) the 5% worst conurbations in terms of the proportion of males who are unemployed or sick are Clydeside, Merseyside, Tyneside, S.E. Lancashire and W. Yorkshire;

(h) the 5% worst conurbations in terms of the proportion of females who are unemployed or sick are Clydeside, Merseyside, Tyneside and S.E. Lancashire;

(i) the 5% worst conurbations in terms of pensioner households are W. Yorkshire, Clydeside, Tyneside and S.E. Lancashire, and

(j) the 5% 'worst' conurbations in terms of the number of children under 14 in a household are Clydeside, Merseyside, W. Midlands and Tyneside.

Taken together, these indices indicate a tendency for 'deprivation' on one criterion to be found with 'deprivation' on other criteria within enumeration districts.

Turning now to the proportion of ethnic minorities from the New Commonwealth, these data show that:

(i) the 5% 'worst' conurbations in terms of the proportions of NC immigrants are the ILEA boroughs, W. Midlands, outer London and W. Yorkshire;

(ii) the 5% 'worst' conurbations in terms of the *concentration* of NC immigrants within enumeration districts are Clydeside, Tyneside, W. Yorkshire and S. E. Lancashire.

Indeed, Clydeside has the smallest number of immigrants but they are most highly concentrated within enumeration districts compared with other conurbations. It is significant, in this regard, that the the ILEA trations in the London area do not come up to the 5% cut-off point.

(iii) when four separate indicators — lack of bath, over-crowding, lack of basic amenities and living in privately rented accommodation — are combined, the proportions of enumeration districts with the highest spatial concentration of these characteristics are the ILEA boroughs, Clydeside, West Midlands, West Yorkshire and S.E. Lancashire.

Taking these data together, then, it is clear that not only is there a correlation between deprivation on one index and deprivation on other indices but that the spatial concentration of indices of deprivation tend to correlate with (a) the proportions and (b) the spatial concentration of ethnic minority communities of New Commonwealth origin. This is brought into sharp relief when the settlement patterns of these communities in the conurbations is taken into account as in Table 1.

TABLE 1: Settlement Patterns of New Commonwealth Born Persons in Conurbations

Conurbations	Total Population	NC% of Tot.Pop.
Great Britain	1,157,170	2.1
England and Wales	1,126,405	2.3
Scotland	30,765	0.6
Tyneside Conurbation	5,010	0.6
West Yorkshire Conurbation	55,485	3.2
Merseyside Conurbation	9,040	0.7
South Lancashire Conurbation	46,690	2.0
West Midlands Conurbation	120,725	5.1
Greater London	476,535	6.4
Outer Metropolitan Area	106,290	2.0
Central Clydeside Conurbation	10,345	0.6

Sources: CRC *Ethnic Minorities in Britain: Statistical Data,* 1975, fifth edition and *Census* 1971 (HMSO), Tab. 2.

This shows a clear tendency for ethnic minority communities to be found in the South-East especially in the Greater London conurbation, the West Midlands conurbations and the West Yorkshire conurbation. This is because they were attracted to these areas in search of employment when they first arrived into the country.

In short, the data indicates that the geography of urban despair incorporates indigenous people as well as members of ethnic minorities from the New Commonwealth. It also demonstrates that to the extent that ethnic minority communities are not randomly distributed throughout the country, the geography of urban despair tends to coincide with the geography of immigrant settlement and concentration within the conurbations. To this extent, the emphasis in recent White Papers is not without substance.

This clearly raises a number of questions which our project was designed to clarify such as: To what extent is urban deprivation perceived by ethnic minority communities? To what extent is the deprivation they experience the result of their immigrant background — language problems, racial discrimination, different religious and cultural backgrounds — or the result of the same factors that contribute towards deprivation among indigenous people in areas of urban deprivation? These questions lead on to another series of questions concerning the extent to which general provision for urban deprivation can incorporate and meet the needs of ethnic minority communities and the extent to which special provision is needed. All these questions turn on the general issue as to whether their needs are similar to or are different from those of indigenous people living in areas of urban deprivation.

Outline of This Volume

In the next chapter, we discuss the outcome of our review of the employment situation of ethnic minority communities in the country as a whole as well as in the conurbations in which they have settled. We then proceed to discuss our findings in connection with Housing, Education, Youth facilities and the Social Services. Methodological issues such as the selection of the eight areas in which the study was conducted, the selection of samples within each one of these areas, the administration of the interview schedules and the phasing of the whole project are described in the Appendices.

Summary

In this chapter, we reviewed policy initiatives which have been adopted by Central Government for dealing with urban deprivation and pointed out the difficulties which are involved in defining the concept of 'urban deprivation' in abstract, academic terms. We also discussed the rationale which informed these initiatives in order to describe the contextual background of this inquiry.

Chapter Two: Employment Patterns of Ethnic Minority and Indigenous Communities

The Significance of Employment

It could be argued, and with considerable justification, that the issue of employment is the most crucial determinant of the state of community relations in the country as a whole as well as in the conurbations where most ethnic minority members have settled. This is because it is bound up with the daily basis of life of the community as a whole and with the expectations of members of ethnic minority communities who decided to settle in those areas where they could find employment. It is also crucially important because it clearly reflects the attitudes of the host community to immigrants who seek employment in order to maintain themselves and their families.

By contrast, the issue of education is a matter which is crucial for the future of community relations because it determines, to a large extent, the attitudes which the second generation of immigrants as well as indigenous children will develop and exhibit when they move out into the wider world at the end of their period of formal education. In this sense, education can be said to be crucial for community relations and especially for the attitudes of the host population in the long term whereas the issue of employment is of more immediate concern not only for the welfare of the indigenous community but also for the welfare of immigrants who now constitute a small but unevenly distributed proportion of the total population of the country.

Largely for this reason, the issue of employment has evoked widespread interest and concern among various research organisations, government departments and among leaders of industry and, indeed, immigrant organistions. Many reports have been published which demonstrate the extent to which ethnic minorities differ from their indigenous counterparts in terms of their industrial location, possession of skills, unemployment and socio-economic status.

This concern can be best illustrated by looking at the sorts of jobs which are undertaken by both indigenous and ethnic minority group workers in the country as a whole.

There are undoubtedly many local characteristics of the conurbations in which ethnic minorities are found (e.g. the structure of industries, the predominance of manufacturing industries as against white-collar and service occupations etc.) which impinge on the employment patterns which are found among these workers. The national approach we adopt in the following pages will undoubtedly under-play the significance of such local characteristics. However this approach has the advantage of enabling us to concentrate on the overall national patterns that apply to both indigenous and ethnic minority workers even while making allowances for such local characteristics. If anything, this approach is likely to under-state the level of disadvantage which ethnic minority workers in any particular town or city experience rather than exaggerate it.

Apart from this, there are four kinds of technical difficulties involved in such an exercise which should be mentioned at the outset. The 1971 Census records information about the country of origin of heads of households as well as statistical information about the economic activity which is undertaken by all those who were resident in the British Isles during Census night. However, every Census since 1961 has been shown to under-estimate the numbers of ethnic minority people in the U.K. for reasons connected with their style of life — e.g. multi-occupation, the greater geographical mobility of those in private tenanted accommodation etc.[1]

Secondly, the information in the 1971 Census is already out of date in view of changes which have taken place in the economic climate in the country as a whole since that time and their impact on levels of unemployment especially, but not only, among ethnic minority workers (which we detail below).

Thirdly, the use of the country of origin of the head of household as a classificatory variable in the Census is likely to lead to an under-estimation of the number of black people whose parents were themselves born in the U.K. but who experience many of the disadvantages which are usually experienced by more recent New Commonwealth immigrants.

This makes it impossible to determine the proportions of U.K.-born persons who are coloured in the country as a whole but especially in areas with long settled black populations such as Liverpool and Cardiff. This problem is compounded by the fact that a 'mixed' marriage in which the head of the household was born of New Commonwealth parents is likely to be classified under 'New Commonwealth' and vice versa depending on the place of birth of the father or mother in such a marriage. The net effect is that the black British population is 'lost' between the classificatory variables which are employed in the Census.

Fourthly, only part of the available information on employment of New Commonwealth immigrants has been published. Somewhat fuller, though even less up to date, information about the range of occupations and employment of ethnic minority workers is available from the 1961 and 1966 Census on which we shall draw to supplement such information as is available in the 1971 Census. For all these reasons, caution must be exercised in extrapolating from the national trends which we discuss below to the specific situation which obtains in any particular town or conurbation.

Economic Activity* Rates: Indigenous and Ethnic Minority Workers

One of the most well-established facts about immigrants in Britain as well as in other countries is that they tend to consist of relatively large proportions of males who are economically active partly because the very fact of immigration establishes a process of self-selection which ensures that it is mostly those who can fend for themselves who emigrate from their countries of origin and partly because the demographic structure of the population of this country has been changing in such a way that the proportions of elderly people have increased faster than the proportions of those who are economically active.

The age distribution and economic activity of ethnic minorities compared to the rest of the population are presented in Table 2.

TABLE 2: Age Distribution and Economic Activity Rates of Ethnic Minorities

Age in Years	NC Born %	NC born in Employment %	NC born Unemployment %
15-19	2.9	2.2	2.8
20-24	3.4	2.7	3.8
25-29	3.0	2.5	3.4
30-34	3.6	3.6	4.8
35-39	4.6	4.9	6.2
40-44	4.0	4.1	5.5
45-49	2.9	2.9	4.3
50-54	1.9	1.9	2.9
55-59	1.4	1.4	2.4
60-64	1.0	1.0	1.5
65-69	0.8	0.8	1.0
70-74	0.6	0.8	1.1
75-79	0.5	0.6	0.7
80 & above	0.4	0.5	0.5

Note 1. The basis for these tabulations are the rest of the population, the total of those employed and the total of those unemployed respectively.

Source: OPC&S *Census* 1971: Advance Analysis op. cit. Table 2, p. 103.

This shows clearly that the ethnic minorities from the New Commonwealth are

---

*'Active' refers to those who are either employed, are unemployed but seeking work (ie registered) or temporarily off work because of ill-health.

virtually absent among the retired population of the country and tend to be concentrated mainly in those age groups which are either economically active or are students. In this regard, it is significant that the proportions of ethnic minorities from the New Commonwealth reach a 'peak' among the 30 to 44 year olds.

Their higher rate of economic activity is brought into even sharper relief when the proportions they constitute in each age category are compared to their representation among those in employment and among the unemployed. As the table shows, they are fully represented among those in employment above the age of 29 years in every age category. However, they tend to be 'over-represented' among the unemployed (compared to the proportions they constitute of the population as a whole) from about the age of 20-24 years — a position of disadvantage compared to the rest of the population. Their distribution 'peaks' between the ages of 30 and 44 and falls off as retirement approaches. More up to date figures about unemployment have continued to reflect this tendency for them to be 'over-represented' among the unemployed. Indeed, all available information about unemployment since 1961 has demonstrated that ethnic minorities tend to be harder hit by unemployment compared to others[2] and that periods of recession exacerbate this tendency so much so that one researcher resorted to the use of a very graphic metaphor by saying: "when Britain sneezes, Walsall catches pneumonia — but Walsall's black workers catch double pheumonia" [3] To what extent do these data on employment and unemployment differentially affect males and females among the ethnic minority groups as compared with the indigenous population?

The 1971 Census provides a clear illustration of the tendency for both males and female workers from ethnic minority groups to be more economically active than their representation in the total population would have led one to presume. Leaving aside those who are still involved in education (e.g. students) and those for whom information about sex was not supplied, there is a

TABLE 3: Economically Active Ethnic Minorities by Sex

	Males %	Females %
NC born as % of total population of both sexes	2.4	1.9
NC born as % of the economically active in the population	2.8	2.3
Total Active of both Sexes in Population (N7	15,713,315	9,170,365

Source: OPC&S *Census 1971: Advance Analysis:* op.cit. Table 2, 102-107.

tendency for members of ethnic minority groups to be over-represented among those who are in employment (especially between the ages of 30-44) as well as among those who are unemployed (in all age groups up to 65). Table 3 illustrates this over-representation of both sexes among the economically active in the population.

But when employment and unemployment are taken into account, their over-representation is brought into even sharper relief as Table 4 illustrates.

TABLE 4: Ethnic Minority Over-representation Among the Unemployed by Sex

| | Males | | Females | |
	Employed	Unemployed	Employed	Unemployed
NC born Actives	2.8	3.3	2.2	3.6
Total Actives	14,870,280	834,035	8,660,695	509,670

Source: OPC&S *Census 1971* op.cit. pp 102-107.

While both sexes are over-represented among both the employed and the unemployed, females reflect a clear tendency to be more affected by unemployment than males. This trend has been worsened by the recessionary trends in the economy since 1975 and a recent study by the Department of Employment has shown not only that unemployment among all black workers increased from 2.2% of the national total in November, 1973 to 3.4% in May, 1975 but that this rate of increase is twice as large among black female workers.[4]

However, the overall activity rates for ethnic minority workers compared to indigenous workers conceal variations between different ethnic groups. When such variations are taken into account, a number of differences emerge which reflect not only the varying composition of these groups in relation to the total population but also reflects a tendency for some groups to be more affected by unemployment than others.

Table 5 illustrates the relationship between the representation of each group in the population as a whole and their representation among those who are economically active. It shows that the proportions of each category of New Commonwealth-born residents who are economically active do not differ substantially from their representation in the total population though there is a tendency for Indians and West Indians to be over-represented among those who are active. When these activity rates are further analysed in terms of the sex of workers and of those who are unemployed, these differences are exacerbated. New Commonwealth born males tend to be over-represented among all active males who are in employment (except in the case of Africans and those from other countries) and West Indian females are notably over-represented among all females in employment while Pakistani females are under-represented.

TABLE 5: Activity Rates of Ethnic Minorities by Sex Compared to Their Representation in the Population

| | *Males* | *Sex of all Actives* | | *Females* | | |
	NC born as % in Pop.	*NC born actives as % of Actives*	*Empl.*	*Unempl.*	*Empl.*	*Unempl.*
India	0.6	0.8	0.9	0.8	0.6	0.9
Pakistan	0.3	0.3	0.5	0.5	0.1	0.2
W. Indies	0.6	0.8	0.7	1.1	0.9	1.6
Cyprus	0.1	0.1	0.2	0.2	0.1	0.1
Africa	0.3	0.3	0.3	0.4	0.3	0.4
Other Countries	0.3	0.2	0.2	0.2	0.3	0.3

Source: *Census 1971* op.cit pp 102-7.

Similarly, West Indian females are most notably over-represented among all females who are unemployed. Indeed, they are twice as likely to be out of a job as to be in one. In sum, unemployment would appear to hit West Indians harder than it hits any other group and to hit the West Indian female harder than it hits any other group of females.

Our analysis of activity rates so far illustrates a clear and systematic difference between ethnic minority workers as a group and the indigenous population. While ethnic minority workers as a whole are not only in those age categories in which they are likely to be at their most productive (in terms of the average life-cycle) but are also available for work, nevertheless they experience a systematic pattern of disadvantage in the area of unemployment. In other words, they are significantly more likely to be unemployed compared to their counterparts among the indigenous population.

We have based our analysis of activity rates so far on the total national figures available for the country (Great Britan) as a whole. However, these national figures are likely to under-estimate both the activity rates and the unemployment rates which ethnic minorities experience in different regions because the ethnic minority population is not evenly distributed throughout the whole country, and indeed, throughout all areas (rural and urban areas).

On the contrary, they tend to gravitate towards centres of employment in the urban areas and are thus drawn into the total workforce available in conurbations. Further, the greater availability of jobs in some regions/conurbations attracted them in increasing numbers to these areas since the end of World War II. When this uneven pattern of ethnic minority settlement is taken into account, the impact of their activity rates and their unemployment rates is exacerbated. Table 6 illustrates their distribution among the active, employed and unemployed population respectively in these areas.

TABLE 6: Settlement Patterns, Activity Rates of NC-Born in Conurbations

Conurbs.	NC % of Tot. Pop.	NC % of Tot. Actives	NC % of Tot. Employed	NC % of Tot. Unemployed
Tyneside	0.6	0.6	0.7	0.7
W. Yorkshire	3.2	3.8	3.7	6.5
Merseyside	0.7	0.9	0.9	1.0
S.E. Lancs	2.0	2.4	2.3	3.4
W. Midlands	5.1	6.1	6.0	9.0
Gt. London	6.4	8.0	7.8	10.9
Out. London	2.0	2.3	2.3	3.1
Scotland	0.6	0.5	0.5	0.4

Sources: CRC *Ethnic Minorities in Britain: Statistical Data,* Nov. 1974, p. 6 and *Census 1971,* op.cit Tab. 2.

It is interesting to note from this table that while New Commonwealth-born persons constitute about 2.1% of the total population of the country, they constitute much larger proportions in some conurbations than in others. Thus they constitute 6.4% of the population in the Greater London area and only 0.6% of the population in Scotland. However, when their uneven distribution is compared to their activity rates, their unemployment rates in some conurbations (e.g. Greater London, W. Midlands and W. Yorkshire) stand out in sharp contrast thus suggesting that the pattern of disadvantage in unemployment to which we have referred affects ethnic minorities in some conurbations to a much greater extent than can be accounted for by their representation in the total population of these areas. The 'worst' conurbations for unemployment among ethnic minority groups are clearly Greater London, W. Midlands and W. Yorkshire in that order.

Occupational Distribution
But if the above analysis, and especially of unemployment, is illustrative of the

disadvantage which minority groups experience compared to the rest of the population, the spread of the actual jobs that they do as well as their industrial status and socio-economic position is even more illustrative of the extent to which their needs differ in the field of employment. Unfortunately, the information which is available on these aspects of employment is not as up to date as one would have wished, since the analyses of these aspects of the 1971 Census have not yet been published. However, some indication of their spread throughout the occupational distribution of the country is available from the survey of British Race Relations which was undertaken by the Institute of Race Relations in 1969, which relied heavily on the information provided by the 1961 and the 1966 Censuses.

This indicates that there are no overwhelming concentrations of ethnic group workers in any indusy (except Cypriots in the clothing and allied industries in the London area). In the West Midlands, on the other hand, it shows that one-fifth of the males of each New Commonwealth group are labourers and that this proportion rises to one-half for Pakistanis, most of whom work in engineering and allied trades (see Table 1a in the Appendices) — a clear contrast with the relatively even spread of ethnic minorities in the London area.

It also shows that the sex distribution of ethnic minorities is largely similar, with Indian-born females being well represented in clerical and professional jobs in the London area and West Indian women in service occupations; Cypriot females are exceptional in being located largely in the clothing trade. By contrast, West Indian women are largely found in engineering occupations in the West Midlands area.

These trends in the occupational distribution of ethnic minority workers are accentuated when they are compared with the occupational distribution of the indigenous population. Such a comparison shows that male Africans and Asians are over-represented and West Indians are under-represented in clerical and professional occupations in the London area compared to the indigenous population. In the West Midlands, by contrast, all male groups of ethnic minority workers, especially Pakistanis, were over-represented among labourers (see Table 1b in Appendices). Indeed, a survey by the PEP confirms that Pakistanis are still vastly over-represented in manual and unskilled jobs compared to the indigenous population throughout the country.[5] It showed, for instance, that whereas 18% of the indigenous population are in semi-skilled or unskilled manual jobs, the proportion of Pakistanis doing these jobs is 58%. By contrast, only 8% of Pakistanis as against 40% of the indigenous population are in non-manual jobs.[6] In the middle ranges of the occupational system, it showed that more West Indians are skilled manual workers compared to every other ethnic minority group — a change from 1966 which is worth nothing *en passant*. 59% of West Indians are skilled manual workers as against 42% of the indigenous population and 44% of Indians. However, a significant break occurs between the skilled manual job level and white collar jobs for as a group ethnic minority workers are still largely to be found in manual jobs and are still markedly under-represented in white collar jobs.

For ethnic minority women in the London area, the greatest over-representation in 1969 was as clothing workers in the case of Cypriots and West Indians to a lesser degree. In the West Midlands, on the other hand, Indian-born women were heavily over-represented in engineering and allied jobs compared to indigenous women.[7] However, the (1975) P.E.P. survey showed that not only are minority women more likely to be working full-time as compared to their indigenous counterparts, but that their occupational distribution throughout the country is closer to that of indigenous females — another change from the situation in 1966[8] — though less favourable than males. For example, 41% of West Indian women and 49% of Indian women are in semi-skilled jobs compared to 24% of indigenous women respectively.[9] Clearly, the postion of ethnic minority men is far more depressed compared to indigenous men than the position of ethnic minority women compared to indigenous females.

Industrial Status

The overall and marked under-representation of ethnic minority workers in the higher and well-paid jobs is sharply reflected when their industrial status (i.e. the prestige attached to their jobs in the industrial/occupational profile) is compared to that of indigenous workers. An analysis of the distribution of ethnic minority workers at various points of the occupational distribution was undertaken and presented by the Survey of British Race Relations in 1969 on the basis of information supplied by the 1966 Census of Population.[10] This showed that the industrial status of all ethnic minority workers is less favourable in the West Midlands than in London, and that all ethnic minority group workers constituted high proportions of those in the 'other employees' category, with the singular exception of Cypriots who constituted a high proportion of those in the 'self-employed' category. Similarly, all ethnic minority group workers are under-represented in the 'managerial', 'foreman' and 'supervisor' categories (see Table 3 in Appendices). Taking these date together, it is clear that ethnic minority workers tend to be found at the lower end of the occupational status profile compared to the rest of the population.

Socio-economic Status

The net effect of their marked under-representation in the higher rungs of the industrial status hierarchy and their over-representation in the lower ones is to concentrate ethnic minority workers in the lower end of the socio-economic status distribution. There are seventeen socio-economic groups which are identifiable from the 1966 Census into which people can be allocated in terms of their occupation and their employment characteristics. These socio-economic groups are reducible into a seven-step ranking of the status or prestige of all occupations in the eyes of the community at large. The British Survey of Race Relations, to which we have already referred above, described the outcome of this ranking procedure for the socio-economic status ranking of ethnic minority group workers throughout the country in terms of the information available in the 1966 Census. It shows, perhaps not surprisingly in view of the trends in our analysis above, that ethnic minorities are markedly under-represented in the top three echelons of the socio-economic prestige hierarchy and are markedly over-represented in the bottom end, compared to the rest of the population in England and Wales (see Table 4 in Appendices). Specifically, there was a marked under-representation of ethnic minority groups among professional workers, employers and managers, and among non-manual 'white collar' workers in general both in London and in the Midlands — areas with large numbers of ethnic minority workers as we have seen. Similarly, ethnic minority males were three times more likely to be unskilled manual workers than the rest of the population. The proportions for females in both the Midlands and in London were not as large.[11]

This pattern of status distribution provides considerable substance for those who have referred to ethnic minority workers as the new proletariat but one which is distinguishable by its colour and which undertakes a wide range of employment activities which their indigenous counterparts do not wish to undertake as living standards rise.

The data that we have just discussed is based largely on statistical information available from the 1966 Census; it could consequently be argued that this information is not only out of date but that it over-states the degree of concentration of ethnic minority workers in the bottom rungs of the social and industrial ladder since some ten years or so have elapsed since that Census was undertaken. Unfortunately, more up to date information is not yet available which can be juxtaposed to the above data in order to find out whether their disadvantaged position has improved with the passage of time. Nevertheless, such additional items of evidence as have been available since 1966 have suggested that the position has not been radically changed with the passage of time and that ethnic minority workers today remain the proletariat of colour that they were during the early sixties. For example, a recent survey of black workers in Walsall demonstrated that ethnic minority workers in that area are still markedly under-represented in the top echelons of the occupational status profile and are virtually excluded from extensive sectors of modern industry.[12] Such a conclusion cannot be generalised to cover the whole country since there are undoubtedly specific factors which set Walsall apart from many other cities throughout the country. Nevertheless, it is highly suggestive of a lack of appreciable change in the trends concerning ethnic minority workers and employment. More up to date information on unemployment to which we referred earlier also reinforces this conclusion. If anything, it illustrates that ethnic minority workers are not only more vulnerable to unemployment at the best of times but that they are even more vulnerable during periods of recession in the economy.

A survey conducted by the Community Relations Commission's Reference Division into unemployment among black (especially West Indian) youths in 1974 showed that they were twice as likely to be unemployed as their indigenous counterparts.[13] An even earlier investigation by the Select Committee on Race Relations and Immigration during 1968-69 showed that there was a range of problems which coloured school-leavers experience on leaving school which deserve considerable attention in the future. In view of this, the Survey of British Race Relations in 1969 was understandably forced to the conclusion that:

> "the concentration of coloured immigrants in certain sections of employment and their absence in others, coupled with the fact that there has been little or no change between 1961 and 1966 gives most cause for concern. If this pattern continues into the 1970s, then the assessment that the situation is still fluid and has not hardened into a rigid class-colour or caste-colour structure may well be over-optimistic. The basic problem should not, however, be seen in those sectors of employment that have over-concentrations of coloured immigrants but in those that have few. It is in the occupations and industries where the coloured immigrant is rare or absent that the answers to concentration, lack of achievement, and frustration are to be found."[14]

Such evidence as we have discussed above suggests that this judgement was, indeed, over-optimistic and that the situation of ethnic minority workers in the field of employment has not improved significantly over the past decade. Further, evidence on the attitudes of employers to ethnic minority workers indicate that the attitudinal base which should lead to improvement over time remains basically unaltered.[15]

Some Explanations

The fundamental question that arises from the above considerations is the simple one concerning the reasons for the marked skewness of the distribution of ethnic minority workers in the field of employment which we have highlighted. Why are these workers virtually absent in some fields and over-represented in others? Why has the occupational status profile remained virtually the same over the past decade or so? Why are ethnic minority workers especially much more vulnerable to unemployment at the best of times and so much more vulnerable during periods of recession in the economy? Why are there so few ethnic minority workers in the professional and managerial categories of the occupational hierarchy and so many in the unskilled manual category? Research over the past decade has advanced some explanations which are worth considering since they indicate the extent to which ethnic minority workers differ from their indigenous counterparts not only in the large conurbations of London and the West Midlands, where they constitute significant proportions of the population, but in other conurbations as well where there are fewer.

These explanations can be divided into three main categories for the purpose of our discussion in this chapter. Firstly, there are those explanations which locate the reasons for the skewness of the distribution of ethnic minority workers in the field of employment in factors which are connected with the immigrants themselves. Secondly, there are those explanations which relate to the actions and predispositions of employers and unions as agencies which are fully involved in dealing with labour relations and with the process of industrial production. Thirdly, there are those explanations which relate to the interaction between immigrants and employers or unions and spread out into the general area of public attitudes. It is as well to discuss each one of these three sets of factors separately even though they are all intimately connected with each other.

Factors Concerned with Ethnic Minorities
One of the explanations which have been advanced (in this category of explanations) for the marked skewness in the distribution of ethnic minority workers in the field of employment concerns the under-developed backgrounds of the countries from which they emigrated. It is argued, in this regard, that the majority of immigrants in the United Kingdom come from countries in the New Commonwealth which are largely agrarian and, in other respects, non-industrial. They therefore lack the advantage of having lived in a country with an industrial background, a country that would have demanded various technological and academic skills from them. Consequently, they come to Britain with those skills which are appropriate to a rural/agrarian society and therefore find it impossible to compete on equal terms with the indigenous citizens of the country as far as employment is concerned, except in the lowest rungs of the occupational hierarchy where their non-possession of industrial skills would be of little consequence. Further, and where they do come into the country with skills, their skills are more likely to be applicable to peripheral aspects of the British industrial economy such as carpentry, cabinet-making and woodworking etc. This, it is felt, is an important reason for their location in the lower rungs of the occupational hierarchy in Britain.

There is very little hard evidence against which this explanation can be evaluated since the 1971 Census does not provide any indication of the backgrounds from which ethnic minorities come other than their countries of origin. However, it seems highly unlikely that this explanation can account for their low position in British society since there are larger numbers of members (3.2% against 2.1%) of ethnic minorities who possess university degrees[16] so much so that many people have expressed serious concern about their *under-employment*[17] in jobs which are lower than their qualifications merit. Further, it is unlikely that their over-representation in the unskilled manual categories of the occupational distribution bears any logical or statistical relationship to the proportions among them who come from industrial/urban backgrounds as against those who come from purely agrarian rural backgrounds. In any event, there is considerable evidence that, firstly, the proportions of members of ethnic minority communities who are still coming into the country as 'immigrants' has considerably decreased as a result of changes in immigration legislation since 1962. In 1964, for example, some 53,000 people from the New Commonwealth entered this country for permanent settlement of whom over a quarter were holders of employment vouchers who were entitled to bring in their relatives and dependents. By 1974, this figure had been reduced to some 22,000 holders of work permits (for temporary residents).[18] By June 1975, only 2,240 people from NC were accepted for settlement.[19] Such legislation would have systematically reduced the proportions of people from agrarian/rural backgrounds who would find it difficult to fit into any part of the occupational hierarchy other than at the bottom since it is mostly those with skills who would be issued with employment vouchers. Indeed, about two out of every five coloured person in Britain today was born here. Clearly, the time is not very far away when the majority of the coloured population in this country would be British and black.

Secondly, evidence from some conurbations which have had a long-standing black British population suggests that their experience of employment and especially unemployment is not only very different from that of their indigenous colleagues but that the positons which they have achieved in the occupational distribution are no different from those which the 'immigrants' proper have had to accept. Several studies from the Merseyside conurbation, for example, have indicated that the bane of coloured (but British) youths in that conurbation is the problem of unemployment and the disadvantage that is associated with that.

Thirdly, there is increasing evidence that having an industrial/cultural background *and* having achieved all the skills which are required for an industrial society do not reduce one's chances of being absorbed into the industrial occupational hierarchy only at the bottom rungs. Roger Ballard and Bronwen Holden of the SSRC Research Unit on Ethnic Relations, for example, found that coloured university students who were born and educated in Britain are at a considerable disadvantage in obtaining jobs commensurate with their qualifications compared to their indigenous counterparts with similar qualifications.[20] Similar information indicating that some ethnic minority students do as well as their indigenous counterparts[21] but experience similar difficulties in employment, suggests that 'employability' is not just a function of the skills possessed by candidates nor is it a function of the industrial or non-industrial nature of the backgrounds from which they derive. Indeed, there is a strong suspicion among many adult immigrants that far from their educational qualifications and skills being a passport to a choice of employment, they very often have the reverse effect since they suspect a tendency for racial discrimination and rejection to be higher, the better one's qualifications and skills are.[22]

A second explanation (in this category) which has been advanced for the marked skewness of the occupational distribution of ethnic minority workers compared to their indigenous counterparts is similar to the above but has evoked a separate approach from policy-makers and therefore deserves to be treated separately. This is the argument that ethnic minority workers tend to be deficient in their use of the English language and that this deficiency makes it difficult, if not impossible, for them to operate at those levels in the occupational/industrial hierarchy in which language skills are at a premium.

There is little doubt that there are large sections of the ethnic minority communities for whom the English language is, at best, a 'foreign language' in the sense that it is not used in the home. Even in the case of those groups, like West Indians, who were born into the English language, its use tends to be very different from main-stream English because it is a 'creolised' dialect which is used not only in the home but also in the wider industrial sphere as well as in schools. For these reasons, various schemes have been instituted in schools as well as in factories (pathway schemes) which are aimed at providing language instruction for ethnic minority communities.[23] To be sure, these schemes have only recently been introduced and affect relatively small segments of those ethnic minority group members who require them. They are therefore unlikely to radically affect the overall language deficiency of ethnic minority groups as a whole in the short run even if it were correct to suppose that to be a member of an ethnic minority community is to be deficient in the English language.

However, and the potential effect of these schemes aside, the ethnic minority communities who have settled in this country since the early sixties reflect such a wide range of knowledge of the English language that it is highly unlikely that this could singularly account for their over-concentration in those jobs which are at the bottom end of the occupation/industrial hierarchy. Besides, some of the evidence we have mentioned above concerning British born and British educated members of ethnic minority groups and the difficulties which they experience in securing jobs commensurate with their skills, qualifications and proficiency in the English language makes it highly unlikely that a general deficiency in the English language can be a valid reason for the skewness which we have observed or, indeed, for the presumption that such a general deficiency characterises anything other than a specific segment of ethnic minority workers. Such evidence as is available from the PEP survey of ethnic minorities shows that on average Pakistanis are likely to be the least fluent in English, East African Asians the most fluent and Indians in between (there is no data for West Indians)[24] but that in every one of these cases, the men are more fluent than the women. Further, the older they are, the less likely they are to be fluent in English; 55% of Asian men and 82% of Asian women who are older than 45 years of age speak little or no English. On this evidence, there is undoubtedly a case for expanding English language teaching schemes especially among workers who are older than 45 years of age.

However, we have seen that ethnic minority workers are over-represented among those who are active in the population between the ages of 30 and 44 years of age. Further, it is well-known that earnings and promotion prospects increase up to the age of 45 and decline thereafter. Finally, the PEP survey mentioned above showed that Asians with qualifications tend to be fluent in English and that the distribution of qualifications among Asians is similar to that of the indigenous population and marginally better.[25]. Where the distribution for Asians differs markedly from that of the indigenous population is when their qualifications are cross-tabulated against the level of the job which they do — indicating a clear tendency either for their qualifications to be discounted or for them to be employed in jobs which are lower than their qualifications merit. Thus, they would (like other ethnic minorities) still have been markedly over-represented in manual jobs even if they all spoke English to an extent which is comparable with their indigenous counterparts. In any case, our demonstration of the similarity between the occupational distribution of ethnic minority women and their indigenous counterparts and the finding that more Asian women are deficient in English than Asian men, (speaking it slightly or not at all), should indicate that language deficiency does not completely account for the marked skewness in the occupational distribution of ethnic minorities which we observed above. It is understandable therefore that the recent PEP survey should conclude that:

"...language competence is unlikely to be a significant factor accounting for the comparatively low job levels of minority men with academic qualifications. ... there is a very strong relationship among Asians between fluency in English and academic qualifications; in fact, this relationship is so strong that nearly all Asian men with degree-equivalent qualifications speak English fluently. Yet it is among this very group that we find the greatest disparity between the level of qualifications and the level of the job.[26]

Factors Concerned with Employers/Unions

Another category of explanations which has been advanced for the markedly skewed distribution of ethnic minority workers in the occupational distribution relates to the composition of the labour force in various areas. One of the most popular variant of these explanations suggests that the composition of labour in a factory is likely to reflect the composition of the labour force in the locality in which that factory is based. Since ethnic minority workers are not evenly distributed throughout the country, employers go on to argue that they are more than likely to be absent in the workforce in factories in those areas in which they are relatively few, and present in factories in those areas in which large numbers of them have settled. If this is so, it would explain why there are some industrial sectors in which ethnic minority workers are under-represented and other sectors in which they are over-represented.

However, the difficulty with this explanation is three-fold. Firstly, the over-representation of ethnic minority workers in the lower sectors of the occupational hierarchy is common throughout the country as we have seen and all the conurbations which we have described exhibit a more than proportional degree of over-representation of ethnic minority workers in the bottom rungs of the occupational hierarchy even though there are more white collar jobs in some (e.g. London and the West Midlands) than in others.

Secondly, there are large sectors of industry in which ethnic minority workers are virtually absent even though these industries are located in areas with high ethnic minority settlement. For example, Dennis Brooks demonstrated that the virtual absence of ethnic minority workers in several industries in Walsall cannot be accounted for in terms of the ethnic composition of the workforce in that city. Similarly, the over-concentration of ethnic minority workers in the metal industry and allied trades in that city cannot be accounted for by the over-abundance of ethnic minority workers in that area. Clearly, the ethnic composition of the workforce available in any particular locality is not a sufficient explanation for their under-representation as well as their over-representation in industries which exist in the same area. Understandably, various studies of this aspect of disadvantage in employment have arrived at the uniform conclusion that the markedly skewed distribution of ethnic minority workers in the occupational distribution in the country cannot be accounted for either in terms of the search and recruitment mechanisms which are employed by employers[27] or, indeed, by the ethnic composition of the workforce which is available in any particular area.[28]

Thirdly, it presumes that the process of recruiting workers is unaffected by the attitudes of the employers. Indeed, the available evidence indicates that employers and unions exhibit attitudes which are antipathetic towards the employment of coloured workers not only in terms of whether or not they should be recruited but also in terms of their tendency to project their own

46

personal attitudes on to their workers in their assessment of ethnic minority workers' potential for promotion. For example, many independent researchers have demonstrated that many employers not only 'anticipate' resistance from white workers to working with coloured labour and therefore avoid recruiting them, but also interpret various groups of ethnic minority workers in terms of their own stereotypical conceptions about West Indians or Indians irrespective of whether they had had experience of working with a coloured labour workforce or not. David Smith, for instance, found many employers among his sample who thought that West Indian workers are slower and less conscientious than whites and West Indian workers more than Asians.[29] He also found employers who thought that Asians are interested in promotion but that West Indians are not irrespective of how long they may have worked for the same employer.[30] He also found employers who do not ever expect to have coloured supervisors in their establishments.[31] Similarly, Patterson found several employers who exhibited what she called a 'wog-complex'; that is employers who were predisposed towards the 'I commanded coloured soldiers during the War; I know how to handle them'[32] kind of comment, indicating a clearly stereotypical orientation towards coloured workers in any conceivable future situation.

Yet these attitudes are rarely expressed openly except where they are projected on to other workers who are thus made to appear to be the real stumbling block to the recruitment, dispersal and promotion of ethnic minority workers. For example, a study undertaken by the Department of Employment found several instances in which employers adopted a 'we have no problems here' approach to the problem of ethnic minority workers in industry only to add, in the same breath literally, that "we have nothing against coloured people. They are alright on certain jobs. There are some here, but we can't see them making much progress." A similarly poignant example of how unconscious employers can be of their own racial discriminatory attitudes towards ethnic minority workers was: "we don't believe in a race relations policy. All our work people are treated alike and the less said about racial differences the better".[33] An equally explicit example of how the process of mental projection of attitudes on to others operates is illustrated by the employer who responded to the Department of Employment's researchers by saying: "we see the need for doing something but if we promote a coloured man to supervisor, say, we'd have a walk-out. We can't afford to run the risk of disrupting production".[34]

These attitudes are not confined to employers but are also shared by trade unionists and even shop stewards on the shopfloor. David Smith provided a clear illustration not only of the extent to which these attitudes are shared by employers and trade unionists but he also cited instances in which there was open connivance between employers and trade unionists in a firm in excluding ethnic minority workers from certain plants and in restricting their promotion on the supposition that white workers would be displeased otherwise.

This tendency to project antipathetic attitudes to other people was once put in a satirical context by the Jamaican poet A. G. Bennet when he wrote:

"Since I come 'ere I never met a single English person who 'ad any colour prejudice. Once, I walked the whole length of a street, looking for a room, and everyone told me that he or she 'ad no prejudice against coloured people. It was the neighbour who was stupid ... Neighbours are the worst people to live beside in this country."[35]

A similar tendency to project antipathetic attitudes to other people is evident in the field of employment in the form of a fear of white workers' resistance. To be sure, white workers have been shown by various researchers to express antipathetic attitudes towards ethnic minority workers to the extent of demanding separate canteen facilities, washroom facilities etc. But such resistance is often exaggerated by employers and trade unionists because of the process of mental projection to which we referred above. Indeed, there is increasing evidence that resistance from white workers tends to disappear where employers take a firm stand on matters which facilitate the employment of ethnic minority workers or where unions come out firmly in favour of non-discrimination at a national level.[36]

It may be thought that since employers and trade unionists are unaware of the extent to which they project their own antipathetic attitudes to other workers, that they are also unaware of the provisions of the 1965, the 1968 and the 1976 Race Relations legislation which prohibits discriminatory practices in employment and in public places. In fact, both the earlier PEP study (reported in Daniel op.cit) and the later one undertaken by David Smith showed that even where employers were conscious of the provisions of legislation, they nevertheless adopted various roundabout methods of avoiding them and thus frustrate the spirit of the legislation.

Yet almost all the available evidence to date suggests that a state of peaceful co-existence exists in industry between employers, trade unionists and white workers on the one hand and ethnic minority workers on the other to the extent that the latter accommodate themselves on the lower rungs of the occupational ladder. Indeed, Dennis Brooks' study of London Transport shows that this state of peaceful co-existence and accommodation can be found alongside antipathetic attitudes towards specific groups of ethnic minority workers. He shows, for instance, that while West Indians are most fully accepted within London Transport (an organisation with considerably more experience of employing them than most), they are nevertheless the object of considerable antagonism.[37] He also shows that they were at a serious disadvantage in relation to promotion until structured and more objective mechanisms were adopted for assessing the suitability of workers for promotion; Smith also shows that this generalisation holds true for a wider range of industries. Invariably, the more informal and subjective the personnel procedures which are adopted in an industry are, the more discrimination ethnic minority workers would experience in that industry and the more favourable would be the treatment which its white workers would receive. By contrast, the more formal and objective the procedures are, the less would be the discrimination exhibited against ethnic minority workers in personnel and promotion assessment.[38]

The Interaction Between Factors Concerned with Minority Groups and Public Attitudes Towards Racial Discrimination

It may be presumed that the attitudes which we have outlined above are operative only within the employment sector. On the contrary, considerable evidence has now been accumulated to indicate that these attitudes form part of a general complex of antipathetic attitudes which are found in other spheres of life (housing, education, etc.) and in the wider society. This complex consists of a range of attitudes extending from strong rejection of persons of colour to a mild rejection of persons who derive from outside of the orbit of this society. Many studies have shown that 'foreigners' who are white are the object of many of the antipathetic attitudes we have described above. Sheila Patterson, for instance, demonstrated that Italians, Hungarians and to a lesser extent Poles have all experienced rejection from employers and from other people in the wider society though she found that coloured workers were the object of more frequent expressions of such antipathy.[40] She also found a tendency for rejection to vary inversely with the colour-shade of the worker such that Indians and Pakistanis experienced less rejection than West Indians but more rejection than Poles, Hungarians and Italians.[41] Other studies have, in fact, suggested that colour-shading among West Indians is similarly correlated with the rejection which is experienced.[42] But by far the major line of demarcation would appear to be the distinction between white and black such that black persons experience more rejection in a wider sphere of life than white persons of 'foreign' birth.

It has been suggested that this complex of attitudes is ameliorated somewhat by propinquity between blacks and whites such that those whites who live or work with blacks are more tolerant than others. This was one of the most significant findings of the Survey of British Race Relations in 1969[43] and had been shown to be the case in the United States some years earlier in spite of the many differences which exist between the race relations scene in the USA and in the U.K. This augurs well for the future especially in view of our demonstration that the majority of the black population in this country in the near future would have been born and educated here and would thus have contributed, by their very presence in the population, to a greater degree of tolerance among their indigenous colleagues than would have been possible otherwise. It also augurs well for the future in view of our demonstration that white resistance tends to disappear where employers, union leaders and central government departments give a clear lead and refuse to cave in to the demands of white workers who are antipathetic towards their coloured colleagues.

However, this finding rests on the presumption that the complex of attitudes inherent in colour prejudice is a function of the minority groups that exist in this country, be they of 'foreign' birth in the case of Hungarians, Poles, Italians and others or of New Commonwealth origin (and therefore black). To the extent that these attitudes are based on stereotypes about these minority groups, this is true; and many studies have outlined the range of stereotypes which are held by the general population of these groups. The Select Committee on Race Relations and Immigration highlighted the dangers of over-generalisation which these stereotypes lead to in 1969 when it said:

"It is dangerously easy to create stereotypes: to see all people of a group or race as one type and not to recognise the wide range of their character and abilities. Some stereotypes have become widely accepted. Because some West Indians have poor education, it is assumed that most West Indians are of low intelligence. Because an employer first encounters an immigrant employee who did not work well, he decides that all immigrants are lazy. Because some Asians lack good English it is assumed that Pakistanis and Indians are unqualified for skilled employment. Many employers have found immigrants as hardworking and steady as any other workpeople."[44]

It cannot then be denied that the task that public education should deal with over the next decade is to eliminate the stereotypes which people hold of ethnic minority groups, for in the last analysis what people believe to be true is true for them in all its consequences and predisposes them to such action as they believe to be correct in the light of the 'truth' that they know. This is the reason why employers take such action as we have seen to restrict the recruitment of ethnic minority workers in the field of employment or to frustrate their aspirations for promotion once they have been recruited. The result of such action is the over-representation of ethnic minority workers in the bottom rungs of the occupational hierarchy as we have seen.

Nevertheless, the presumption that propinquity (at home or at work) between whites and blacks tends to increase tolerance rests on the further assumption that stereotypes of disadvantaged groups cannot exist in the physical absence of such groups or cannot precede their presence. This is an important consideration to which sufficient attention has not been directed in Britain for there are many areas in the country in which very small proportions of ethnic minorities have settled and other areas in which they are completely absent. Policymakers have presumed that those who have not had contact with ethnic minorities either in their places of work or in the places where they live are not likely to develop negative stereotypes of these people by virtue of that fact. They have therefore gone on to presume that the problem of public education for tolerance is one which should be dealt with in the towns, cities and conurbations where ethnic minority workers have settled over the past two decades, oblivious of the possibility that ethnic minorities are likely to disperse to other areas over the next two decades as their economic and social circumstances improve.

The research evidence available suggests not only that negative stereotypes of groups can be entertained by persons who have had no contact with the 'disadvantaged' group in question but that such stereotypes can also predispose such persons to adopt antipathetic attitudes towards a group as well as to groups which do not exist at all.

In this connection, one of the most exciting pieces of research on this involved an experiment with subjects who were asked whether they would object to having various minority groups as their co-citizens (i.e. living in their town), as their neighbours (i.e. living next to them), as their guests and as their prospective in-laws (i.e. marry into your family). These various possibilities were arranged in a series of increasing circles of proximity and intimacy. The list of ethnic groups in this experiment included three non-existent, 'non-such' ethnic minorities (viz: Danireans, Pireaneans and Wallonians — not to be confused with Walloons). It is significant, in the context of our discussion, that the subjects in this experiment expressed varying degrees of antipathy towards various existent groups but were generally antipathetic towards non-existent groups as well. What this experiment illustrated vividly is the way stereotypes can operate even in the physical absence and, indeed, non-existence of ethnic groups. Clearly, the task of public education cannot be confined to either a limited group of persons such as employers and other people like them who are in a position to discriminate against ethnic minorities but must also involve those who live and work in close proximity to ethnic minorities as well as those who do not, those who are in a position to discriminate as well as those whose careers have not yet taken them to such heights.

In this respect, it may be thought that the finding from the Survey of British Race Relations that only about 10% of the indigenous population are strongly prejudiced and only 17% are inclined towards colour prejudice is significant for it would appear to suggest that the task of public education needs to be focused on this minority. Further, the passage of time since that Survey was undertaken and the amount of public education which has already taken place (through radio, television and the press) would have made some inroads into the proportions of those who can be said to be significantly prejudiced among the population. Yet, there is continuing and up-to-date evidence which indicates that the situation has scarcely changed in this respect. For example, studies of colour discrimination in recruitment for jobs continue to indicate a tendency for employers to discriminate against those who appear to have names that usually belong to members of ethnic minority groups. Daniel conducted employment tests with Pakistanis, Indians and West Indians on the one hand and English and Hungarian applicants on the other and found that the former groups were systematically discriminated against at the job recruitment stage;[45] Hungarians were also less favourably treated than English applicants. David J. Smith,[46] like Ballard and Holden,[47] found that coloured applicants had to make more applications for jobs than their English counterparts; and these studies were all undertaken in 1966, 1973 and 1974 respectively using subjects who all had British qualifications and (in the case of Ballard and Holden) had been born in Britian and received all their education in this country. McIntosh and Smith also found that white 'foreigners' (e.g. Italians) were also still the object of antipathetic attitudes in 1974.[50] A further study undertaken for the CRC in 1975 which dealt with members of the black British population in Liverpool also convincingly demonstrated that persons of colour are discriminated against at the recruitment stage in 30% of all applications made for jobs — the same figure of 30% which McIntosh and Smith found in their survey.

TABLE 7: Public Opinion Polls on Attitudes Towards Coloured Immigrants in July 1973, May 1974 and November 1974
"Would you say that in this country the feeling between white and coloured people is getting better?"

	1973 July %	1974 May %	1974 Nov. %
Getting Better	24	30	25
Getting Worse	33	23	29
Remaining the same	35	42	38
Don't know	8	5	8
	100	100	100
Base	1,022	1,132	1,111

Sources: Louis Harris International *Speedsearch* (unpublished).

The consistency with which this figure of 30% has turned up in various surveys is cause for pessimism especially when this is juxtaposed to several public opinion polls conducted for the Community Relations Commission which show that many people are themselves pessimistic about the state of community relations between whites and coloureds. Table 7 shows that people think that the situation has remained virtually unchanged throughout the period from 1973 to the end of 1974. Subsequent polls have presented similar results except in 1977 when respondents reflected the extensive political discussion about coloured immigration which took place then by a feeling that race relations are getting worse.

Nevertheless, the figure of 30% which has been consistently shown to be involved in studies of discrimination at the recruitment stage is ironically also an optimistic note of some sort for it does suggest that the majority of the population are not prejudiced against ethnic minority communities and that there is a 'hard-core' of people who occupy positions of power in which they can bring their antipathy towards coloured people to bear in the employment field. If 70% of the population are tolerant, or are inclined towards tolerance then the most important problem for public education in the future is to reach out to the 30% who are either strongly prejudiced or are inclined towards racial prejudice.

This conclusion is reinforced by the finding that few people believe that coloured minorities should be treated differently when applying for jobs in spite of the fact that they are discriminated against and in spite of the fact that the people who express this view are themselves somewhat pessimistic about the state of race and community relations in Britian today. For instance, the Speedsearch public opinion Poll conducted in November 1974 included a question on this particular issue.

TABLE 8: Public Opinion Poll on Attitudes Towards Discrimination Against Coloured Applicants in the Field of Employment
"Should coloured applicants be treated differently for jobs?"

Response Categories %	Responses %
Differently	13
Same	82
No Opinion	5
	100
Base	1,111

As Table 8 shows, no less than 82% felt that they should be treated in the same way. The same Speedsearch survey also shows similar responses on related questions concerning whether coloured people should be treated differently for council housing allocation, for admission into pubs and clubs, and in selecting school places for their children.

It would appear from our discussion then, that antipathetic attitudes towards ethnic minorities are not restricted to the field of employment but are found outside of that limited sphere as well but that, in general, the majority of the population are basically tolerant whereas only a minority are either strongly prejudiced against ethnic minorities or are inclined towards such prejudice. It is this minority specifically who would have to be the prime (but not the exclusive) target of public education programmes over the next two decades.

Summary

The evidence we had adduced in this chapter strongly suggests that not only are antipathetic attitudes towards ethnic minority communities found amongst a minority of people but that these people are invariably in a position to exercise their attitudes against the interests and fair treatment of ethnic minorities thus placing them at a distinct disadvantage compared to their indigenous colleagues in the urban areas in which they have settled. This is the basic reason for the under-representation of ethnic minority communities in the middle to upper ranges of the occupational hierarchy. There are, to be sure, other contributory reasons which we have highlighted viz: the lack of leadership by union leaders at national level and by employers, poor language skills among some immigrant workers, the agrarian/rural nature of the background of the countries from which some of them emigrated and so on. Nevertheless, the most widespread reason for their under-representation in the middle to upper ranges of the occupational distribution is, in fact, the existence of negative stereotypes of racial and ethnic groups which are exercised by those who are in a position to discriminate in the field of employment.

In the chapters which follow, we shall demonstrate that there is a similarly considerable difference in the situations of ethnic minorities in urban areas and their indigenous colleagues as far as housing, education and the social services are concerned.

Chapter Three: Patterns of Disadvantage in Housing and Housing Allocation

There is an absolute sense in which it can be said that housing is in short supply relative to the demand for it from all sections of the community and that all low income families have been in a seriously disadvantaged position as the degree of competition for scarce resources of housing increased since the end of the Second World War. In this regard, it can be maintained that the failure of successive governments to build the required amount of dwellings at prices which most people can afford, the fact that the waiting lists for council housing in the inner city areas has not been significantly reduced over the past decade, the fact that housing provision (both private and public) has been at the mercy of the vagaries of different political ideologies and the constraints which they have had to contend with,[1] the fact that inflation in recent years has put house prices outside the reach of most people including many of those who are in the upper socio-economic groups, have created serious problems for all sections of the community alike.

Indeed, private rented accommodation (both furnished and unfurnished) has declined steadily since 1947, helped along by changing economic conditions as well as by government legislation, to the disadvantage of those sectors of the population who were heavily dependent on it, especially in the South East where multi-occupation has always been greater than anywhere else in the country. Their plight has been made steadily worse by the fact that other kinds of housing tenure have not increased by an amount which is commensurate with the decline in private rented acommodation. Table 9, for instance, shows not only this steady decline but also shows that whereas

TABLE 9: Changing Patterns of Tenure in England and Wales: 1947-1971

Tenure of Dwellings	1947	1961	1966	1967	1971
	%	%	%	%	%
Owner Occupier	27	44	49	50	50
Public Authority	12	25	27	27	28
Privately rented etc.	61	31	24	23	22

Source: Ministry of Housing & Local Govt. *Council Housing: Purposes, Procedures and Priorities,* London: HMSO, 1969 Table 1, p.5 & *Census* 1971.

private tenanted accommodation declined from 61% of all housing tenure in 1947 to 22% in 1971, public housing increased from 12% in 1947 to 28% in 1971, and owner occupied dwellings increased from 27% in 1947 to 50% in 1971. Thus, if even the characteristics of people living in all types of tenure were the same, displacement of persons in the privately tenanted sector has increased much faster than the ability of the other two sectors to absorb them.

However, while this situation affects most people and while it is true, as a consequence, that housing is in short supply for most people, it is nevertheless, also true that some groups are worse off than others for a variety of reasons which we shall outline. In this chapter, we shall be concerned with the relative disadvantages of ethnic minority groups in this situation compared to those of the indigenous population in order to demonstrate that (a) these groups are relatively worse off in absolute terms as well as in terms of the extent to which they form part of sub-groups within the population who are at a disadvantage in the housing field e.g. the homeless; (b) they have relatively higher degrees of housing need in terms of the quality of housing which they live in and the conditions which apply in those houses; (c) the allocation mechanisms incorporated in the private housing market as well as in public housing tend to:

(i)   discriminate against ethnic minority groups and

(ii) discriminate in favour of the indigenous population, in ways which cannot be accounted for by reference to their housing needs even though local authority officials especially, as well as building society executives, often declare that their policies are applied to all those in need of housing without reference to their origins, religion or skin colour; and

(d) there are cultural and demographic factors at work among members of ethnic minority communities which influence their housing need and predispose them to operate in the relatively more depressed end of the housing market.

In order to carry out these objectives, it is as well to examine the household composition of ethnic minority communities and their earnings and to compare them to those of the indigenous population. This will serve to demonstrate that while there is a relationship between gross income and the quality of housing which people can afford, this relationship is not such a straightforwardly simple one that the latter can be predicted from knowledge of the former. We can then go on to examine the distribution of ethnic minority communities across all classes of housing tenure and compare it with that of the indigenous population in the context of our earlier demonstration that ethnic minorities tend to be concentrated in the conurbations in general and in inner city areas within these conurbations in particular. We then go on to discuss some of the mechanisms which have contributed to these distributions and the findings from our survey with 'decision-makers' in housing.

Household Size and Dependents

Since the size of a household is crucial in determining the kind of dwelling which is appropriate for a family, it is as well to begin by observing that the average size of ethnic minority households has always been higher than that for the indigenous population. This was the case in 1966[2] and remains so today. The 1971 Census showed that the average household size for the general population in England and Wales is 2.8 people. On the other hand, the General Household Survey showed that the average household size for ethnic minority communities is 3÷71 (3.81 in Census 1971) persons whereas that for the indigenous population is 2.78 persons — a significant difference. The PEP Survey of Racial Minorities (1975) came up with even larger average figures (partly as a result of a different basis of sample selection). Even if one were to allow for greater sampling errors in the latter survey, the difference between the household sizes of ethnic minority communities and the indigenous population is still significantly large. Table 10 shows the distribution of different household sizes among various ethnic minority groups.

TABLE 10: Average Household Size Analysed by Country of Origin and Religion

Asians and West Indians only	All Household members	Adults aged 16+	Children aged 0-15	Base
Asians and West Indians (All)	4.76	2.59	2.17	1,828
West Indians	4.31	2.16	2.15	735
Asians (All)	5.19	3.00	2.19	1,093
Pakistanis	4.96	2.90	2.06	410
Indians	5.20	2.94	2.26	468
African Asians	5.33	3.39	1.94	2.5
Moslems	5.13	2.82	2.31	571
Hindus	5.29	3.25	2.04	253
Sikhs	5.70	3.22	2.48	205

Source: *PEP Survey of Racial Minorities* op.cit. P.55.

This shows that the average household size for West Indians and Asians is 4.76 but that West Indians have an average household size which is below this figure whereas all Asian groups have an average household size which is above this figure. Indeed, Sikhs have the largest average household size of 5.70 persons.[3]

Such large families are accounted for, firstly, by the fact that the majority of ethnic minority persons are in their reproductive phase as we stressed earlier when considering their age distribution compared to the indigenous population. They accordingly have more children per household than the indigenous population. Thus 77% of all ethnic minority households contain children under the age of 15 as against 47% of all households in the country.[4]

Secondly, such large families are accounted for by the number of adults they contain. According to the 1971 Census, there are 2.25 adults per household in the general population but, as can be seen from Table 10, all Asian groups (but not West Indians) contain more than this number of adults. Few of these adults are aged 60 or over. Indeed, the indigenous household is three times more likely to contain elderly people than the ethnic minority household (4.6% as against 13.6%)[5] as a consequence of the different age distributions of both groups. These differences in household sizes clearly necessitate more spacious dwellings, all things being equal, compared to the indigenous population. To what extent does their earnings profile enable them to obtain such dwellings as are commensurate with the sizes of their families and households?

Earnings and Dependants

Little reliable information is available on the gross incomes of all sections of the community which would enable us to undertake a comparison between the incomes (from all sources) of ethnic minority workers and indigenous workers. However, the PEP survey of Racial Minorities provided a comparison of gross earnings between ethnic minority workers and indigenous workers which indicates that the latter earn more on average than the former. The median gross earnings, according to that survey, for indigenous workers is £40.20 per week whereas it is £36.70 for all ethnic minority workers.[6] When the distribution of earnings among minority workers is compared to their occupational distribution, there is a relationship between job levels and gross earnings; but the greatest disparity between the gross earnings of ethnic minority workers and indigenous workers appears at the top end of the occupational distribution in which, it will be recalled, the former workers are markedly under-represented. Similarly, when gross earnings are compared to the age at which full-time education was completed, ethnic minority workers are worse off than their indigenous colleagues. In other words, the relatively lower levels of gross earnings of ethnic minority workers is a reflection of their marked concentration in manual jobs which *a fortiori* are not as well paid as are white collar and professional jobs. To this extent, they are at a disadvantage (relatively) in the competition for housing on the open market to the extent that such competition is dependent on earnings.

In this regard, it may be thought that their larger families and households would contain persons who are not dependants but who are able to contibute towards the income of the family. This is a reasonable supposition since, as we have seen, more ethnic minority women work full-time than their indigenous counterparts.

However, the evidence from the PEP survey suggests that ethnic minority women who are working cannot contribute significantly to the family purse because their earnings are lower than those of their male relatives even though there are few inequalities in *their* (i.e. female) distribution of gross earnings compared to that of their indigenous counterparts.[7] Indeed, the gross earnings of all women (ethnic minority and indigenous) are lower than those for all men. It is perhaps therefore understandable that not only do ethnic minority workers receive the earnings which they do receive but that they are also more likely to work 'permanent night shifts' and day shifts in order to raise their median gross earnings by a meagre £1.30 or so[8] per week. Indeed, the gross earnings coming into an ethnic minority household are likely to be depleted because these households have, on balance, more dependants than wage-earners even though, as we have seen, they contain fewer elderly persons as well as more wage-earners compared to indigenous households.

TABLE 11: Dependency Ratios for Households for Whites and Minorities by Country of Origin of Head of Household

	(b) *Average No of working adults*	*(a)* *Average No. of dependants*	*(a/b)* *Dependency*
Asians & West Indians	1.91	2.99	1.57
West Indians	1.73	2.57	1.49
Pakistanis/Bang.	1.83	3.16	1.72
Indians	1.84	3.44	1.87
African Asians	2.03	3.35	1.65
Whites	1.46	1.70	1.17

Source: PEP "Survey of Racial Minorities" op.cit. p. 67 & 68.

Table 11 shows the dependency ratios (calculated by comparing the average number of dependants per household with the average number of wage-earners per household) for each minority group. Asians and West Indians together have a higher dependency ratio (1.57) than the indigenous population (1.17); and all Asian groups have even higher dependency ratios, with Indians having the highest compared to the indigenous population. Clearly, the greater the number of dependants in a household, the worse off would that household be in terms of disposable income.

On this analysis, Asian and West Indian households, but especially Asian households, are worse off than indigenous households in terms of gross earnings. Their earnings from their full-time employment is therefore unlikely to enable them to effectively compete on the open market for the type of accommodation which would be appropriate to their family size and household sizes. How then do they make out in the private housing market as well as in public housing? What is their distribution across various types of housing tenure compared to the indigenous population?

Housing Tenure Among the Indigenous and Ethnic Minority Populations

One of the most remarkable contrasts between ethnic minority housing tenure and that of the indigenous population concerns the proportions of the former who are owner-occupiers. Table 12 below compares the distribution of Asians and West Indians among the various housing tenures with that of the general population.

TABLE 12: Tenure: West Indians, Asians and the General Population

	West Indians %	Asians %	General Population %
Owner Occupied	50	76	50
Rented from Council	26	4	28
Privately Rented	24	19	22
Not Stated		1	
Base	4,303	4,784	

Source: PEP *Survey of Racial Minorities* and *Census* 1971.

The distribution of West Indians is similar to that of the general population but that of Asians is very different with 76% living in owner-occupied housing and only 4% in council housing. This is all the more remarkable when it is juxtaposed to the marked over-representation of all ethnic minority workers among manual workers as we have seen and to the fact that there is a correlation between owner-occupation and the higher socio-economic groups in the general population, with 77% of professional/management workers in owner-occupation as against 20% of unskilled workers.

From the occupational distribution of ethnic minority workers, one would have expected Asians to be more fully represented among council tenants all things being equal. But neither the Survey of Racial Minorities nor the General Household Survey found this to be the case. Indeed, when the job level of heads of households among ethnic minorities is compared to their housing tenure distribution, there is a marked tendency for Asians who are manual unskilled workers to buy their own homes, more often on leashold and more often in areas of Asian concentration compared to both West Indians and the indigenous population.[9] By contrast, non-manual Asians are more likely to live in privately rented housing even though, as a group, ethnic minorities are over nine times as likely to live in privately rented dwellings (19.6%) compared to the indigenous population (2.3%).[10]

The reason for this reversal of the distribution among Asians as compared to other groups is partly related to the fact that they exhibit a strong desire to own their own homes, wishing equally strongly to avoid becoming council tenants,[11] and partly because their household and family size predispose them to buy the larger but older Victorian-type houses in the inner city areas which are relatively cheap and somewhat inexpensive compared to property which was built after 1940. The PEP Survey of Racial Minorities found that owner-occupation is correlated with high concentrations of immigrants and low availability of council housing. Thus owner-occupation does not have the same connotation for ethnic minority groups as it does for the rest of the population since it reflects an attempt to obtain appropriate accommodation for relatively larger households and families at prices which they can afford.

This finding is brought into even sharper relief when the quality and cost of owner-occupied housing among ethnic minorities is compared to that of the indigenous population. Taking the basic structure of the building as an indicator of its quality, the PEP survey found that whereas 21% of the indigenous population live in detached houses, only 1% of the ethnic minorities do; whereas, on the other hand, only 30% of the indigenous population live in terraced houses, 66% of ethnic minorities do. Similarly, 52% of the indigenous population live in houses which were built after 1940 whereas only 10% of ethnic minorities do. On the other hand, 24% of the indigenous population live in houses which were built before 1913 whereas 46% of ethnic minorities do.[12] In other words, ethnic minority communities are almost twice as likely to be living in houses which were built before 1913.

In terms of other criteria of quality, ethnic minorities are worse off compared to their indigenous counterparts. They are markedly over-represented among those who live in shared dwellings, almost ten times as likely to be sharing baths and almost six times as likely to be sharing WC and over twice as likely to have 2.50 persons per bathroom compared to the indigenous population. When all these facts are taken together, the predilection for owner-occupation among groups of ethnic minority communities falls into perspective: it indicates that ethnic minorities are at a disadvantage in the open market for private owner-occupied housing partly because their incomes are low and partly because their requirements for larger housing cannot be easily met by the housing stock which is available to them.

One would have therefore expected a greater demand from them for public housing because of their obvious housing need but their cultural predilection for owner-occupation as well as the fact that they are often disqualified by the allocation procedures for council housing (e.g. terms of residence before qualifying for admission to waiting lists, eligibility criteria such as nationality and other factors[13]) means that they tend to be under-represented among council tenants (19% ethnic as against 32% of indigenous population). To be sure, their demand for public housing is likely to increase as increasing proportions qualify for admission to local authority waiting lists and as clearance schemes in inner city areas demolish their housing. Further, as leases run out on their properties, they are increasingly likely to be dispossessed and then have to turn to local councils for public housing.

But even in the case of those who are now living in council housing, the evidence, and it is a growing body of evidence, suggests that they experience disadvantages in that sector of the housing field compared to their indigenous counterparts, quite apart from the vicissitudes involved in the allocation procedures to which we have referred. 10% of West Indian and 18% Asian council tenants are living in shared accommodation compared to 0.6% of indigenous council tenants; they are also more likely to be living in flats (48% as against 17%) and to be living in pre-war public housing estates (75% as against 38% of indigenous council tenants).[14] Yet, they pay the same rents as do their indigenous counterparts for what is effectively inferior accommodation. In the sphere of private rented housing, ethnic minority tenants pay almost double for accommodation, invariably to ethnic minority landlords who would have bought their houses at great cost in order to let out rooms in order to recover their costs and thus contribute to the density which characterises the housing which ethnic minorities enjoy. Such landlords, to be sure, perform a useful function from the point of view of local authorities.[15] Public health 'control' orders, prosecutions of miscreant landlords, government legislation as well as clearance schemes in inner city areas have all contributed to the general reduction in private tenanted housing since 1947; this has increased the demand for public housing from ethnic minority communities as well as for owner-occupation.

However, immigrants do not feature only as landlords of often over-crowded lodging houses, they also feature as sellers and buyers of inadequate types of owner-occupied dwellings. This is especially true of Asian groups who live in areas of concentration within the inner city. For Asians, and especially for those who speak English only slightly or not at all, there are positive advantages in living in a community of their cultural compatriots. The PEP survey, to which we have referred, found that there is a correlation between being unable to speak English fluently and living in areas of concentration — a relationship which is stronger among Asians than among any other ethnic minority. By contrast, there is an equally strong relationship among Asians between being able to speak the

English language fluently and living outside of areas in which Asians are concentrated.

This relationship is reflected in the tendency among Pakistanis especially to work 'permanent nights' with mostly other Pakistani workers and fits in with the tendency for Pakistani women especially to stay at home more often than women from any other ethnic minority group. In effect, living in areas of concentration of similar ethnic minorities provides the ethnic minority immigrant with a community of people who share the same language, culture and religion and who are thereby enabled to 'make out' by withdrawing themselves from the main gamut of British social life as far as possible. Largely because of this, there is a premium for living in areas of concentration especially among Asians. The result is that separate private housing markets have emerged for particular ethnic minority groups to cater for both buyers and sellers of property in some northern areas. The premium for living in areas of concentration as well as the need for larger houses has been shown to contribute a sizeable disparity between the valuation of houses in inner city areas and the actual selling/buying prices. To this extent, ethnic minority communities who live in areas of concentration compete against each other and drive up the prices of the inadequate houses which are available — a situation which compounds the disadvantages for those who are buyers[16] in such areas.

The question which arises from this consideration concerns the reasons why ethnic minority communities should place a premium on living in areas of concentration even though the economic disadvantages are such that they push up the prices of their homes by competing against each other for such accommodation as is available. There is no doubt that community pressures constitute a significant 'pull' factor especially among those who wish to withdraw from British social life either because they are not fluent in English or because they are in a strange environment i.e. the 'immigrant syndrome'. There is equally no doubt that the need to live near their places of work and recreation, a factor which has been mentioned by some commentators, also constitutes a 'pull' factor. They however, do not sufficiently account for it since there have been other immigrants who exhibited a similar desire to live near to their compatriots — Jews in the East End, Poles and Hungarians in Croydon etc. — during their early years of immigration but who have now dispersed from the areas in which they initially settled even though they still maintain their cultural and religious ties with their communities.

The analysis of the 1971 Census by Lomas and Monck suggests, however, that while considerable movement has taken place among ethnic minorities between 1966 and 1971, that such movement is limited to the local authority boundaries in which they have originally settled[17] rather than across local authority boundaries even though the ethnic minority communities they examined contain people who immigrated into the country a long time ago. Certainly, the Pakistani munity in Bradford is a community of long standing in the area. The 'pull' factors are therefore not sufficient to account for ethnic concentrations; there are also 'push' factors operating within the society at large which force ethnic minorities to take refuge among their cultural compatriots which are not as clearly understood.[18] We discuss some of them later in this chapter (e.g. anticipation, as well as actual experience, of racial discrimination).

What, in effect, our analysis of patterns of disadvantage among ethnic minorities in the housing field has shown so far is that while housing is problematic for the population as a whole and while inflation may have increased the difficulties of obtaining a roof over one's head by driving house prices above levels which most people can afford — problems which ethnic minorities face as well as the indigenous population — nevertheless there are systematic disadvantages over and above these which affect minority groups especially. Faced with inadequate incomes for their households which are larger, faced with the need to provide accommodation for themselves which needs to be larger, conveniently arranged and located for their friends in their communities, immigrants who are owner-occupiers adapt themselves by obtaining inadequate accommodation at high prices or increasingly turn to their local authorities for public housing.

Some explanations
We have already seen the contribution which large families, large households and a large number of dependants per wage-earner makes to disadvantage in the field of housing. However, it would be a mistake to presume that these are the only significant reasons which contribute to the disadvantage of ethnic minorities in this field. Other equally significant reasons have been advanced which require to be considered in this discussion.

One such explanation concerns the way the institutions which regulate access to housing and the mechanisms which they operate, work to the often unintended disadvantage of ethnic minority groups. In the field of private housing, building societies and local authorities are the two most significant agencies for providing finance for house purchase. Both institutions have always prided themselves on their social functions in assisting households which have housing need. Building societies specifically have emphasised this aspect of their operation especially in relation to first-time buyers even before the recessionary and inflationary trends in the economy became as strongly evident as they were in 1976. Yet, the available evidence suggests that local authority finance has been far more useful to ethnic minorities who are interested in owner-occupied dwellings than building societies. For example, the PEP Survey of Racial Minorities found that local authority provided mortgages were more significant for ethnic minorities living in owner-occupied properties than building society mortgages. Whereas 73% of indigenous people living in owner-occupied properties obtained building society mortgages, only 43% of Asians and 51% of West Indians obtained their mortgages from this source. By contrast, 15% of Asians as compared to only 4% of the indigenous population obtained their finance for house purchase through a Bank loan — a method of finance which is very expensive and allows for a much shorter period of repayment than both building society mortgages and local authority mortgages. Similarly, whereas only 13% of the indigenous population living in owner-occupied dwellings obtained their mortgages from local authorities, 33% of Asians and 39% of West Indians obtained their mortgages from this source. These differences between ethnic minority groups and the indigenous population are surprising especially when the marked predilection towards owner-occupation among Asians is taken into account.

One of the reasons for this concerns not only the patterns of entitlement to mortgages of the various institutions, but also the relatively higher deposits which building societies require of their borrowers for inner city houses, the fact that properties in inner city areas which are bought by ethnic minorities have a lower valuation, are usually in a worse condition, and have a shorter life than those which are bought by the indigenous population. Building societies and banks are least likely to look favourably on advancing money for the purchase of these riskier properties. Even local authorities consider these factors when advancing 100% mortgages — a fact which accounts for the marked under-representation of minority groups of mortgages provided even from this source.[19] In effect, ethnic minorities are caught between the Scylla of low earnings and large families and the Charybdis of having to buy short life properties on leasehold which are in inner city areas out of necessity rather than out of choice. In effect, it is the mechanisms by which finance institutions operate in the private housing market in advancing mortgages which discriminate against ethnic minority communities in the inner city even though such discrimination is not intentional.

Little information is available on intentional racial discrimination by these institutions; however, insurance companies, acting in their role as mortgage guarantors, have been known to discriminate in this as well as in the motor insurance field.[20] It is perhaps therefore understandable that more Asians have had to buy their properties outright compared to other groups in the society. For example, Pakistanis — one of the most disadvantaged groups as we have seen — are more likely to buy their properties outright compared to the general population (33% as against 23%).[21]

A second reason concerns the way the allocation mechanisms for public housing operate to the — again often unintended — disadvantage of ethnic minority groups especially since public housing should correct the inadequate housing circumstances which generally operate in private tenanted accommodation and in some sections of the market for owner-occupied housing, and especially since local authorities are responsible for enforcing public health legislation through the provisions of the Housing Act, 1961.

An extensive study of the allocation mechanisms in ten local authorities undertaken by David Smith and Anne Whalley[22] showed that ethnic minority communities are at a disadvantage in the allocation of public housing for a number of reasons. Firstly, ethnic minorities have to fulfil residential qualifications in many local authority areas before they can be put on the waiting list — a practice which the Cullingworth Committee was highly critical of. 33% of ethnic minority applicants for public housing were on the 'deferred' list against 14% of the active waiting list. Secondly, they qualify on the points system as being in housing need but filter through to the active waiting list only very slowly. Thirdly, they are more likely to fall into categories for priority in housing — such as the homeless — which qualify for such accommodation as is readily available even though such accommodation may be inadequate. Fourthly, the officials who administer the routine aspects of the scheme are more likely to be prejudiced towards ethnic minorities and to assess their house-keeping standards as low. The result is that ethnic minorities tend to be found in pre-war estates more often as a result of the operation of the allocation mechanisms than out of choice. Understandably, they not only are under-represented among council tenants compared to their indigenous counterparts but they also tend to live more densely in flats in estates in the inner city areas. Clearly, such an outcome is more the result of the operation of the allocation mechanisms than of deliberate and intended racial discrimination against ethnic minorities. It is also, in part, the result of the fact that ethnic minorities as immigrants have to gradually enter the 'queue' for public housing. Their representation will undoubtedly increase as they satisfy residence and other qualifications. Nevertheless, these results clearly emphasise the importance of the recommendations of various bodies such as the Cullingworth Committee (1969), the Select Committee on Race Relatons and Immigration (1971) and the Department of Environment's response (in 1975) that constant monitoring on the basis of carefully kept records be undertaken from time to time.

A third reason for the patterns of disadvantage which we have outlined above concerns the operation of racial discrimination against ethnic minorities in the private housing market especially in private tenanted accommodation. No accurate national estimate of the extent of racial discrimination in the private housing field is available. Nevertheless, there is a strong suspicion that estate agents[23] and accommodation agencies have been discriminating against ethnic minorities either by persuading them to buy properties within certain areas (sometime on the advice of property sellers) or by not informing them of private tenanted accommodation with landlords who would prefer other types of tenants. The Race Relations Board investigated a number of estate agents and accommodation agencies who have been known to discriminate in this way.

There is however, no overall estimate of this contribution to racial discrimination against ethnic minorities.

What has been investigated is the extent to which landlords discriminate against tenants from ethnic minorities on the one hand, and the extent to which potential tenants from ethnic minorities avoid indigenous landlords who are likely to discriminate thus artificially restricting themselves to a smaller sector of the market for private tenanted accommodation on the other. The PEP studies of 1967, 1973 and 1975 showed that there is still massive discrimination in private tenanted accommodation and that many members of ethnic minorities (as well as indigenous people) *believe* that there is racial discrimination in this sphere. In the 1967 study, 62% of the West Indians who took part in situation tests experienced racial discrimination on the telephone and 75% on sight. By 1973, discrimination against West Indians had fallen to 27% of all applications.[24] The result of the coincidence of personal experience of racial discrimination and a widespread belief that it occurs is that ethnic minorities exhibit a marked tendency to seek private accommodation from landlords who are themselves members of ethnic minorities — resulting in an almost perfect correlation between landlords and tenant. 47% of West Indians in private tenanted accommodation have West Indian landlords. 45% of Pakistanis in private tenanted accommodation have Pakistani landlords and 53% of Asian tenants in this type of accommodation have either Asian or East African Asian landlords.[25] These tendencies are more likely to increase as the market for private tenanted accommodation shrinks further. Considering that ethnic minorities are still over-represented in this sector of housing, the future of these tenants must lie in public housing via the allocation mechanisms which we discussed above.

To what extent are policy-makers in local authority aware of these parameters of the housing problem as it effects ethnic minorities in their areas? What impact have these parameters had on their conception of their role as Housing Authorities? To what extent have they been constrained in the performance of their role by administrative, political and financial considerations? To what extent do they recognise that there are some respects in which ethnic minorities have special needs as against other respects in which their needs are the same as those of the indigenous people in their areas? These are questions which arise from our discussion so far which our survey of 'decision-makers' was designed to throw some light upon.

Survey Findings

Our survey on Housing was designed after the publication of the PEP study of Race and Housing which had provided much basic background material on the operation of allocation mechanisms within local authorities. That survey, it will be recalled, also provided information on the unintended consequences of these mechanisms for the quality of the housing which ethnic minority tenants of local authorities experience. However, it did not provide information on the extent to which matters such as these as well as those we have outlined above are taken into consideration at the policy-making level. It was therefore felt that a limited survey of issues relating to housing which is focused on the decision-making level (Housing Directors level and at the level of Housing Committees within local authorities) would throw some light on the extent to which these parameters are taken into account in the formulation of policy within local authorities.

Accordingly, the interview schedule which was used dealt with two issues: (a) the role of Housing Departments and Housing Committees and (b) the extent to which differences have been perceived in the housing needs of ethnic minorities and indigenous people living in these areas. The interviews on housing were undertaken with Housing Directors and Chairmen of Housing Committees in all eight project areas as well as with senior officers who operate in the field of Housing e.g. Borough Planning Officers, Directors of Housing, Research and Intelligence officers, Environmental and Public Health Officers, and lasted for an average of one hour.

The Role of Housing Departments

All respondents interpreted the role of their Departments in terms of their statutory responsibility for the provision of accommodation for the population in their areas as a whole. In practice, however, the system of housing allocation ensures that those who are able to provide adequate accommodation for themselves are given low priority as against those who are not able to do so. Consequently, local authorities' responsibility for housing the socially disadvantaged is given higher priority. But our respondents all stressed that no category of the population is either included or excluded by reason of their religion, race or creed; rather people of different religions, race and creed are involved in local authority housing allocation mechanisms to the extent that they qualify as being in housing need:

> "As Housing Manager, I see our role as a Department to meet the overall general housing needs of everybody living in the Borough, with special emphasis upon deprived classes of persons such as the disabled and others."

> "...to improve housing standards both qualitatively and quantitatively thereby improving the standard of life, not just for ethnic minorities but for everybody. They are included in the total view."

> "We provide a comprehensive housing service, with emphasis on catering for every type of class, from the poor-house to the penthouse in theory. In practice, we are concerned less with owner-occupiers in good districts than we are with the deprived private rented sector."

In this regard, considerable dependence is placed on the rationing mechanism of the points scheme and the waiting list. In stressing this, one official pointed out that:

> "Unless we've been asked to investigate a problem to ascertain the points that a person has attained, you will have never seen the person you are offering it to; you wouldn't know unless, of course, it was a Polish name or something like that or a Pakistani name because you get the Smiths and Joneses and even Robertsons from the West Indies. We ask about nationality here; they always put down 'British'. So we wouldn't know."

In terms of their functions then, all respondents saw their role as providing for the housing needs of the population in their areas as a whole with particular emphasis on those who are socially deprived or disadvantaged. This may, but need not necessarily, include ethnic minorities. Where it includes ethnic minorities, this is less because of a conscious focus on them as a particular category of persons and more because they fall into those categories for whom local authorities are generally responsible. Their overall approach then is to make general provision of housing accommodation to all those who are in housing need thus implying that they see no systematic difference between the housing needs of ethnic minorities and those of the indigenous community.

It may be supposed from this, that the very visible presence of ethnic minorities in these areas (as a consequence of their settlement patterns which we have discussed earlier) is entirely ignored by decision-makers and is not allowed to influence the execution of their general responsibility for housing. In order to find out whether this is the case, we asked respondents: "When you are making policy decisions on housing, have you found that these have been influenced by the fact that you have a high proportion of ethnic minorities in your areas? If so, on what issues and with what effect?" It became apparent, very early in the interviews, that few decision-makers had allowed the very visible presence of ethnic minorities in urban areas to colour their general perception of their role as initiators of housing policy. Consequently the majority of respondents were emphatic in their response:

> "The answer is 'No'. Everything depends on the operation of the points system."

> "The question is answered by a very short answer 'No'. It makes no difference at all to our housing points system or anything else. We do not look at the question of a person's skin-colour or anything else."

However, closer probing of the responses to this question revealed that the majority of the respondents were so sensitive about their role as public officials that they were unwilling to allow matters such as this one to influence the determination of policy for fear of being charged with discrimination *in reverse* by the indigenous population in their areas. They consequently not only interpreted their role as decision-makers in the field of housing in a general way but also felt disposed to ignore the, in many cases, very visible presence of ethnic minorities in their areas in spite of the political reactions which this has caused in the past. This general sensitivity towards racial discrimination *in reverse* is marked not only in relation to officials who operate in the field of housing but also among officials in other policy areas.

It could be supposed, to be sure, that this response was a function of the interviewers who conducted these interviews.[26] In order to control for this variable, black interviewers undertook some of these interviews and indigenous interviewers undertook the rest. The result was however invariable irrespective of the interviewers involved. In almost every instance, the responses were the same; the emphasis which respondents attached to their responses did not vary with the racial background of the interviewers.

It is, indeed, notable that very few (only one official in one area in fact) expressed anxiety about being charged with racial discrimination *directly* by members of ethnic minority communities in his area compared to the relatively considerable anxiety which was expressed by the majority of respondents about being charged with discrimination *in reverse*. This is all the more remarkable when it is juxtaposed to the considerable emphasis which respondents placed on the points system as an objective determinant of housing need irrespective of the background of applicants. Clearly, while the housing points system was presumed to be able to cope with whatever charge of racial discrimination may be levelled at them by ethnic minorities, there was a general sensitivity about the possibility of a charge of racial discrimination in reverse arising from the indigenous population which the points system was not presumed to be able to cope with, at least not in the same way. This sensitivity must have precluded open discussion of issues which impinge on or derive from the very visible presence of ethnic minorities in these areas.

However, if this anxiety about the possibility of a charge of racial discrimination in reverse is remarkable, it is equally remarkable that a few senior officials had thought through their role to the implications of the presence of ethnic minorities in their areas though only a minority (two areas) stressed that they had allowed this factor to influence both their discussions of policy and the operation of their Departments. In response to the question mentioned above, one official in one of these two areas stressed that:

"This is causing a problem."

and went on to spell out some of these problems which the presence of ethnic minority communities in their areas have brought to light and to which they have had to give some thought when he said:

"The Improvement programmes for the older, larger Victorian type houses which are very much over-occupied, have to take the extended families of, specifically, Asian immigrants into account. This problem would not have been there and would not have affected our policy-making considerations had the entire population of... (area mentioned) consisted of indigenous people entirely. Similarly, the issue of harassment of tenants is a largely ethnic minority problem to which we have had to give some thought and resources."

He went on to add that:

"We are, as a result, having to increase the numbers of four, five and indeed six bedroom houses on our Housing Programme."

Officials in another area similarly pointed to issues which specifically relate to immigrant groups but not to indigenous people (from the point of view of policy-making) when one of them said that:

"We have had to provide emergency accommodation for battered Asian wives. It is the practice of Asians to beat their wives."

In spite of the unusual way in which the issue of accommodation for battered wives is put, it is clear from this that there was a recognition that the presence of ethnic minorities impinges on policy considerations in a way which calls for some response from policy-makers. Yet another official in the same area recognised that general categories of need can nevertheless impinge more directly on ethnic minorities than on indigenous people even though such categories are not exclusive to ethnic minorities in urban areas when he said:

"The major social deprivation is to be deprived of housing. We have had 51 cases of homelessness in the first three months of this year. If this continues for the whole year, it will be a 50% rise in homelessness this year. A fair proportion, probably an over-representation in relation to the total population, of the homeless are from ethnic minority communities. We do not keep records of the racial background of applicants and so cannot be certain of that figure..."

Officials in this area also stressed that different ethnic minority groups have differing dispositions towards different types of tenure which have to be taken into account in the long term planning of their housing stock. He said in this regard, that:

"We have looked at different patterns of needs and aspirations. We did a survey in an area with a lot of immigrants, asking them where they wanted to live, what sort of house etc. West Indians wanted tenancy or owner-occupation as available but Asians look almost exclusively to owner-occupation. There are very few in council houses and we make no special provision for Asians except as they fall in with the letting scheme. We don't keep records of country of origin in council house lettings....."

These responses indicated an awareness of the extent to which the visible presence of ethnic minority communities in urban areas impinge on policy-making considerations within local authorities.

However, it would be wrong to presume that only a few senior officials were aware of factors such as those mentioned above which either affect ethnic minorities specifically or affect ethnic minority communities more than it affects indigenous people. On the contrary, what our discussion above underlines is the fact that while most senior officials and elected members are aware of these parameters, very few of them were able to highlight their awareness in the context of the policies of local authorities. It is this, in fact, which reflects the extent to which local authority officials are sensitive to the possibility of their being accused of racial discrimination as stressed above. Indeed, most of our respondents felt disposed to reflect only the policy of the local authority within which they operate as they understood it. This policy is, as stated by one official:

"...to ignore race, religion and colour in deciding whether or not a case should be re-housed. And I think this has been a fundamental point in the Council's policy all the time I've been with the Council. When it comes to a question of need, need as related to the factors of housing need, they are not related to any other aspect such as what your religion is, how tall you are, and things like that. So there is no difference in the approach which is adopted towards re-housing an Irishman, a Catholic, a Protestant, a West Indian and so on."

This general policy however appears to have constrained the extent to which senior officials are disposed to take into account various considerations which impinge on the various groups in their areas. There is a serious sense in which it can be said that re-housing an Irishman or a Jew is not the same as re-housing an Asian because there are various considerations pertaining to their needs — the need to be near a place of worship, work etc — which senior officials are aware of but cannot bring to bear, at least not openly in council, on their policy-making considerations.

One such consideration which appears to have been widely accepted as playing an important role is the question of translation of information into the various languages of ethnic minorities in local areas. In this regard, one official said:

"The major deprivation of coloured people is that they are often duped by builders, or have handed over money without proper guarantees. We find that coloured people have not understood buying or grants procedures; they do not understand the housing game."

and went on to discuss various measures which they have taken to make information about these matters available to ethnic minorities.

There were no respondents who did not agree with these sentiments or have not taken steps either to provide information about housing to ethnic minority communities (as well as indigenous people) in their areas or have not translated such information into the various languages of ethnic minorities or do not have translators services available within the areas in which ethnic minority applicants live. However, this was the only issue in connection with which a specific issue pertaining to ethnic minority communities influenced policy-making decisions and was widely debated at the most senior level of policy-making.

In order to explore their awareness of other considerations which are either specific to ethnic minorities or affect significant proportions of them as against indigenous communities in these areas, we asked them: "Have you identified any special housing needs arising from the patterns of family living in different ethnic minority groups? Have you been able to take any steps to meet these needs?" The responses which this question evoked showed that senior officials and councillors were aware of some of the characteristics of ethnic minority communities in their areas even though only those from two areas said that these considerations had been allowed to influence policy-decisions and debates in the local council. As was to be expected, one senior official replied cryptically:

"We do not discriminate in this local authority either for or against ethnic minority groups nor have we considered the possibility of special needs for specific categories of people in our locality."

Another reflected the same sentiments equally categorically when he replied:

"There has been no discussion of this nor can there ever be."

However, other respondents went beyond the framework of policy within their local authorities and raised a number of considerations which they had themselves had to consider in the course of their work irrespective of whether these considerations had filtered through into the policy of their local authorities or not. One respondent mentioned the problem of housing extended Asian families and went on to suggest ways of approaching this problem. He said:

"The problem of housing large extended Asian families is compounded by the very strong bond which exists between newly-married couples and their parents — a bond which disposes these couples to wish to live with their parents in the same household.

This does not apply to West Indians in general. Consequently, the degree of over-crowding among Asians in ... (area mentioned) is marked. One way of informing Asians about the difficulties which this causes for our Housing programme is to set up community organisations, run by ethnic minorities, to act as a buffer and as a channel of communication. But there are no special policies nor have we ever considered a special scheme to deal with this problem or, indeed, the whole issue of special needs."

Others discussed the issue of hostels for young people from ethnic minority groups (not because such hostels are required only by ethnic minority groups but because more young people from these groups are unemployed and homeless than indigenous people in the short term), their greater need for rent investigators, their greater need for housing advice and housing aid, and the problem of single mothers:

"There is a high proportion of single mothers in the West Indian community which causes no problems because we do not discriminate against single mothers in housing; they are dealt with in the same way as married people; we have no problems with single Pakistani males or with large extended Asian families since ... per cent of our development are four-bedroom units which is ample for their needs. Both the Irish and other minorities in this area present these same problems in relation to re-housing or re-development."

One of these respondents mentioned the problem of re-housing Muslim families with more than one wife. Another discussed the issue of providing larger type houses for extended families but had also clearly thought through to some of the practical dilemmas which can arise when considerations such as this one are taken into account by a council which is prepared to modify its general policy to deal with the special needs of particular groups of people. He said:

"Rented accommodation does not meet immigrant aspirations. Therefore if we build large council houses for extended families, they would have to pay very high rents, and would be unacceptable to immigrants. Their aspiration is to become owner-occupiers. Their needs for large units can be met by the large Victorian type houses in the inner city and immigrants can, at the moment, afford them. We examined the cost of building five-bedroom houses. The estimate was very high and the rents we would have had to charge, even after subsidies, would have been in excess of £3,000 per year. This was well above the average for this area. This is, in fact, housing for the rich. This rent would have been much higher than paying a mortgage on the larger Victorian type houses. By giving immigrants mortgages for these types of houses we were able to meet their aspirations and their needs."

He went on to talk about their long history of providing joint mortgages to facilitate the purchase of these houses, stressing that joint mortgages were not confined to house buyers from ethnic minority groups even though they made more use of it. He then suggested that the present cut-back on local authority mortgages are affecting ethnic minorities more than indigenous people because of this and because Building Societies have always steered clear of the larger Victorian type houses in the inner city.

Summary

In sum, our survey of senior officials and elected members of local authorities showed that, firstly, there is a considerable degree of sensitivity towards the possibility of being charged with racial discrimination in reverse by the indigenous population and towards being seen (as public officials operating within public bodies) to consider needs which are either specific to ethnic minority groups or affect large numbers of them compared to their indigenous community. It could have been supposed that this sensitivity would be more marked among elected members than among senior professional staff for political reasons. In the event, the survey showed that both groups were equally sensitive. Largely because of this, most respondents felt disposed to operate within the framework of the policy of the local authority of 'No discrimination' and interpreted the word 'discrimination' in a somewhat narrow and inflexible way.

Secondly, we found that most senior officials and elected members were aware of the broader parameters of housing need among ethnic minority communities in their areas and had, in many cases, thought through to their implications for policy even though these parameters were not allowed to directly determine the policy of their councils. Most of the professional respondents were not only aware of these parameters but had also considered some of the steps which would have to be taken if the needs which they give rise to are to be met in the long term. However, they have either not been able to bring these considerations to bear on the policy of the council or have been prevented by the apparent inflexibility of such a policy from bringing out these considerations during their council's discussions.

One respondent reflected the extent to which his council's policy predisposed him to ignore the question of special needs when he said:

"Once you consider the notion of special needs, you start to determine yourself that there are differences which exist between groups. If you are building your houses to use, it makes no difference at the end of the day who goes into those houses provided they've got a priority to go in there in the first instance."

There is therefore a hiatus between the statutory role of Housing Departments as it influences councils' policy and the private thoughts of senior officials as they go about their daily tasks. In many cases, their extensive experience in the field of housing disposes them to consider various ways and means by which many of the intractable problems they confront in their daily tasks can be dealt with in the long term. However, these are only rarely allowed to emerge in open debate within council meetings. Other constraints which emerged were undoubtedly financial ones especially in the light of the cuts in housing programmes (especially mortgage lending) which are now in force. In this regard, it is interesting that a few of our respondents felt that these cuts are likely to affect ethnic minorities more than indigenous people in their areas. A further constraint was the officer's professional conception of his role as a public official. Some respondents viewed their professional identities in ways which made it difficult, if not impossible for them to consider issues that impinge on one group more than another whereas others viewed this as part of their role irrespective of whether their conceptions of their role was supported by the declared policies of their local authorities.

Thirdly, those respondents who had considered the question of 'special needs' viewed them in terms of (a) needs which are directly related to the characteristics of ethnic minorities and (b) needs which apply to the population as a whole but which affect larger proprotions of ethnic minorities than indigenous people by virtue of their newness, their lack of understanding of the 'housing game' or their cultural dispositions. With the exception of the need for making information available to ethnic minorities about housing in their languages (or making the services of translators available to officers), most respondents viewed the special needs of ethnic minorities in relation to housing in terms of (b) above. Thus, their perception of 'special needs' was a relative one, not an absolute one.

In subsequent chapters, we shall examine the extent to which the hiatus between the declared policy of councils and the professional expertise and experience of senior officers were reflected in the interviews in other areas of policy — education, youth and the social services.

Chapter Four: Policy Issues in Education

We have already established in the previous two chapters that members of ethnic minorities from the New Commonwealth constitute only 2.1% of the total population of the country but that their geographical distribution is such that they tend to be found in the conurbations rather than in the rural areas, in the inner city areas rather than in the suburbs. We have also established that their distribution across occupational categories is such that they tend to be found more often among the skilled, semi-skilled and unskilled manual workers rather than among white collar and professional workers. It will also be recalled that their patterns of housing reflect their relatively low earning power compared to their indigenous counterparts even though their disadvantages in the housing field are more extensive than can be accounted for by their earning power, qualifications or, indeed, activity rates, due to the effect of racial discrimination.

In this chapter, we turn our attention to education and discuss both the policy issues which have been of concern to many people including the immigrants themselves and the findings of our surveys; we shall also discuss the extent to which there are points of difference between ethnic minority pupils and indigenous pupils in British schools in inner city areas. Many of those which have evoked concern are those points of difference which place the ethnic minority pupil in a disadvantageous position compared to his indigenous counterpart and are thus specific to the fact of his being an 'immigrant' in the sense of his being new to this society and to the fact that he is, like his parents, unfamiliar with the British education system. There are, however, others (the 'social class mix' of the schools he attends, his level of achievement within these schools) which are common to both ethnic minority pupils and indigenous pupils from the lower socio-economic groups which we shall highlight.

We stress this distinction between those points of difference which are specific to ethnic minority pupils of immigrant parentage and those which are common to both indigenous children and ethnic minority children in order to emphasise the fact that racial discrimination, where it does operate in the field of education, does not take the direct and bland form which it takes in the field of employment and housing even though education, like housing, is a service provided by local authorities in local areas. This is largely because New

Commonwealth immigrants in the fifties and sixties arrived in the country without their families and invariably sent for them only when adequate opportunities for education, employment and housing had been secured. The mere presence of immigrants during this period, as Bowker has stressed, did not therefore appear to raise any particular educational issues which was felt to deserve special consideration by policy-makers.[1] It is arguable, however, whether some aspects of racial discrimination did not intrude into the early policy considerations concerning the 'ethnic mix' of schools and into the political discussion which preceded and led to the development of a policy on concentrations of ethnic minority children in schools. Nevertheless, many ethnic minority parents believe that it played a part in the process of ascertainment for ESN schools and Bernard Coard[2] suggested that it operates in a systematic way in this regard. We shall go into further details of the way the ESN schools have operated in the past as well as discuss the findings of our survey towards the end of the chapter.

Ethnic Minority and Indigenous Pupils in School: Policy Issues

Partly because of the inherent pattern in New Commonwealth immigration which made it necessary for parents to send for their children only after they had themselves settled in and partly because those who were involved in running the education system were unfamiliar with the sorts of problems that may be involved in dealing with ethnic minority children, points of difference (and indeed similarity) between ethnic minority pupils and indigenous pupils emerged only gradually and were recognised as policy issues eventually. These policy issues did not therefore feature in official discussions of education all at the same time but were recognised as specific investigations were undertaken and as local education authorities attempted to work out practical solutions for dealing with some of the issues which impinged directly on their local responsibility for education. For example, schemes for teaching English as a second language to ethnic minority children have been implemented in many areas where there are immigrants. But these schemes owe their origins to the local attempt of a Headteacher in a local school (e.g. Spring Grove)[3] or a local authority to deal with the low level of proficiency in the English language of ethnic minority children in schools in a particular area. Nevertheless, the policy issues which are outlined below emerged as a result of the constant interaction between local education authorities and central government (especially HMI School Inspectors at the Department of Education and Science).

There are five policy issues which have evoked concern and which indicate the extent to which ethnic minority children in schools are disadvantaged compared to their indigenous counterparts. These are (a) the issue of the numbers of ethnic minority pupils and their concentrations in schools, (b) the issue of their language needs, (c) their achievement patterns and ESN school placement, (d) the impact of the socio-economic background of these children and the issue of their pre-school needs and (e) the contribution of their educational experiences to their sense of identity.

Numbers and Concentrations of Ethnic Minority Pupils in Schools

While ethnic minorities from the New Commonwealth constitute only 2.1% of the total population of the country as we have seen, their children constitute something of the order of 3.3% of the total school population in the country and Townsend and Brittan even suggested that their representation in schools could be even higher if a broader definition of 'immigrant' were adopted. They accordingly suggested that immigrant pupils probably constitute 4.5% of the total school population on a broader definition.[4] While these figures are not large, they nevertheless clearly show that the children of ethnic minority parents are over-represented in the school population compared to their representation in the population as a whole.

However, their over-representation did not cause as much concern as did their uneven distribution across schools throughout the country as well as their distribution across schools within particular conurbations/regions. To be sure, the presence of ethnic minority children in British schools during the early period of immigration (pre-1962) did introduce an element of unfamiliarity into the British school system, which was not geared to coping with the sorts of problems which are involved in teaching children who derive from cultures which are often far removed from those of children in the host society.

This element of unfamiliarity undoubtedly discomfitured some teachers who were not willing to face the prospects of adapting their schools and thereby the education system to cope with the problems involved in teaching immigrant children. The numbers of teachers and educationists who found themselves in this position during the early years of New Commonwealth immigration into the country was however rather few. Consequently, many educationists felt that the problems of educating these children would be solved in time and that the education system would adapt itself to provide for the educational needs of these children in the way that it has always done with previous waves of immigrants from Europe during the early part of this century.[5]

This was undoubtedly a justifiable supposition for most people to hold so long as the numbers of 'visible' ethnic minority children remained at the levels at which they were running at the end of the fifties. As New Commonwealth immigration increased during the early sixties, the numbers of ethnic minority children increased and concern was expressed by politicians, educationists and by parents of indigenous children about the concentrations of ethnic minority children which were then evident in various schools within particular conurbations as well as in some regions as against others. For example, the majority of ethnic minority children were and are still to be found in schools in the South-East, South Lancashire and in the West Midlands. Further, the proportions they constitute varies from 15% of total enrolment in some schools to 75% in others.

According to Little, ethnic minority children constitute 25% of the total enrolment in schools in two local education authorities; they constitute 20% to 25% of total enrolment in schools in five local education authorities and 15% to 20% in a further six. In 1,000 out of 33,000 schools, ethnic minority pupils constitute over 25% of enrolled pupils[6] in 1973. More up to date figures are not available since the Department of Education and Science stopped collecting statistics of immigrant children in schools on the basis of criteria[7] which failed to take into account the increasing numbers of ethnic minority children who are born in England and who do not qualify as 'immigrant children' in the sense in which other ethnic minority children were so referred. It is, however, unlikely that the degree of concentration in schools has substantially declined since a significant number of immigrant children who came into the country before the Immigration Act of 1971 effectively reduced their numbers, are still at school. It was thus the distribution of such children across regions and across schools within particular regions which created concern in the minds of many policy-makers, educationists, politicians and parents.

Julia McNeal is therefore basically correct when she said that the bogey of education for immigrant children in Britain was never the issue of the degree of racial discrimination which they may experience but was the issue of their concentration which was not, to be sure, unconnected with the fact that they are visibly black:

"...the bogey has not been discrimination — less favourable treatment — but concentration. This has been condemned not so much because it might lead to less favourable treatment, but often because it was seen as the development of foreign enclaves within British culture and society.[8]

Though little or no evidence is available to suggest that this concern with concentration was connected with feelings of racial antipathy during the early sixties, nevertheless, it was clearly related to feelings which were engendered at the time by the anti-immigration lobby and by the general suspicion of foreigners which Banton analysed in his consideration of the so-called "stranger hypothesis" as an explanation for racial prejudice and discrimination in Britain.[9]

The view that racial discrimination — less favourable and inferior treatment — was never the bogey of education does not preclude the fact that individual teachers, administrators and, indeed, pupils may have been racially prejudiced either against ethnic minorities or, in the case of ethnic minority children, against each other since they are all, in essence, not systematically distinguishable from their counterparts outside of the education system or from the employers whom we have shown in an earlier chapter to practice racial discrimination in recruitment. Indeed, an interesting study undertaken by Bagley and Verma using attitude scales found that English pupils in 12 schools in multi-racial areas in London and the Midlands (14 to 16 year olds) displayed the most racism while West Indian pupils displayed the least, both towards Asians and towards other groups.[10]

Rather, the view that racial discrimination was never the bogey in the education of immigrant children suggests that it was the issue of concentration which became the point of departure for policy-makers in this field. Indeed, it was the concentration of ethnic minority children in schools in particular areas within cities rather than their concentrations in the conurbations (e.g. South-East, West Midlands) which became the focus of policy. We shall demonstrate, later in this chapter, that while a concern with dispersal as a means of reducing concentrations of ethnic minority children is no longer as widely evident among policy-makers as it was in 1963, nevertheless many policy-makers and professional practitioners (in this case teachers) we spoke to during the course of the study still feel that concentrations of ethnic minority children in schools pose problems for education which policy-makers must continue to take into account even though they differ in the extent to which they feel that dispersal by 'bussing' is the best way of dealing with the problem or in the extent to which dispersal should be undertaken for educational (e.g. remedial/peripatetic reasons, specialised language teaching etc.) as distinct from considerations concerning the racial or cultural background of the children involved (which would necessitate the dispersal of indigenous as well as ethnic minority children).

This concern with concentrations of ethnic minority children in schools, spurred on by a political crisis in 1963 when indigenous parents threatened to withdraw their children from schools in Southall (in which there were concentrations of ethnic minority children because they feared that their own children's educational progress would be impaired) resulted in the issue of Circular 7/65 by the Ministry of Education under Lord Boyle to the effect that local education authorities should endeavour to keep ethnic minority childrens' enrolment in schools down to 30%, thus positing a systematic point of difference in policy between ethnic minority pupils and indigenous pupils of considerable significance.

To be sure, documents incorporating Departmental thinking about immigrant children had been published before the issue of Circular 7/65 and stressed the importance of ensuring that the language proficiency of immigrant children was such that they would benefit from the education system. A

Ministry of Education pamphlet on this subject (*English for Immigrants*) was published in 1963[11] for example. Similarly, the Central Immigrants Advisory Council, set up in 1963 by the Conservative Government of the day to advise the Home Secretary on matters concerning the welfare of immigrants, published its Second Report in which it stressed, among other things, that one of the disadvantages of concentrations of pupils from ethnic minority groups is that it impairs the progress of indigenous pupils by interrupting the normal routine of the school. It added that:

> "There is a further danger that educational backwardness which, in fact, is due to environment, language or a different culture may increasingly be supposed to arise from some inherent or genetic inferiority" (presumably among ethnic minority children).[12]

It went on to suggest that concentrations in schools impair the rate at which immigrant children integrate themselves into the society.

These two documents, published at a time when political concern with stemming the flow of immigrants had not yet subsided (indeed, it is still with us) and at a time when indigenous parents were worried about the effects of the presence of ethnic minority children on the educational progress of their own children, provided the rationale for Lord Boyle's Circular 7/65. Accordingly, Lord Boyle explained the reasons for restricting immigrant enrolment to 30% to the House of Commons in terms of (a) the need to reduce concentrations (b) the need to improve the opportunities for the integration of ethnic minority children and (c) the need to provide concentrated facilities for teaching English to these children and thus improve their proficiency in the language while hinting at the problem that dispersal must imply for children of indigenous parents when he said:

> "...it is desirable on education grounds that no one school should have more than about 30% of immigrants. It is both politically and legally *more or less impossible* to compel native parents to send their children to school in an immigrant area if there are places for them in other schools."[13]

He went on to add, in tones which are only slightly more reminiscent of the Crusader's cry "Jerusalem has fallen" than of political thinking at the time; that:

> "I must respectfully tell the House that one school must be regarded now as *irretrievably* an immigrant school. The important thing to do is to prevent this happening elsewhere.[14]

When the White Paper on *Immigration from the Commonwealth* was published later on in 1965, it reiterated the substance of Circular 7/65 that immigrant children should be dispersed in schools in such a way as to ensure that their concentration did not exceed 30% in any one school and that special language teaching arrangements in schools are provided for teaching them English.

The irony of this, as EJB Rose et al. have shown,[15] is that the earlier 1963 pamphlet had, in fact, called for the bringing together of ethnic minority children for English language classes in one school — a noticeable contradiction to the spirit of both Circular 7/65 and the White Paper on *Immigration from the Commonwealth*. It would appear then that the issue of concentration of ethnic minority children in schools constituted such a significant political and social determinant of policy in education that it over-shadowed the equally important issue of the need — a need specific only to ethnic minority children — to provide specialised and additional language instruction in schools as stressed by the 1963 pamphlet. It thus constituted the most important point of difference between ethnic minority pupils and their indigenous counterparts in schools.

The reactions of local education authorities to Circular 7/65 were mixed: some authorities went on to implement dispersal by 'bussing' children from ethnic minorities to schools outside of the inner city areas where there were more places available; some objected to the fact that only immigrant children were to be dispersed and did not take up dispersal as a policy; some of those who adopted dispersal schemes operated it on strictly educational criteria and others operated it on racial criteria; some applied their dispersal schemes to infants, juniors and seniors in secondary schools and others confined it to juniors and seniors only, objecting to the 'bussing' of infants on the grounds that they were too young for the vicissitudes of daily travel over long distances; yet others found that the objections of teachers in the receiving schools were such that it was difficult to draw up and implement dispersal schemes without rancour in some schools.

No evaluation or monitoring was initially provided for when the dispersal principle was enunciated in Circular 7/65 and no systematic evaluation covering the whole country has been undertaken since. Nevertheless, it would appear from field reports that the wave of objections from ethnic minority parents to that aspect of the dispersal principle which singled out their children for 'bussing', has subsided as some of these parents saw and came to appreciate the additional facilities in the schools to which their children were 'bussed'.

Some local education authorities, on the other hand, found it impossible to keep to the suggested limit of 30% because of the numbers of ethnic minority pupils in their areas who require the facilities for language teaching which are available in the outer city schools to which children were 'bussed'; they consequently raised the limit to 40% of total enrolment. By 1973, one local education authority even found it necessary to exceed this figure and raised the limit even further before deciding to abandon dispersal altogether since the administrative costs of dispersal had by then far exceeded whatever educational advantages it may have had initially. It is likely, indeed, that dispersal by 'bussing' will be abandoned by all local authorities within a relatively short time even though the initial concern with concentrations which led to their adoption schemes remains an important one for largely educational reasons. Besides, the fear expressed by many indigenous parents that their own children's educational progress would be impeded by concentrations of ethnic minority children in schools has not been substantiated by such research investigations as have been undertaken into the relationship between the ethnic mix of schools and the performance of indigenous children.

Little and Mabey's study of reading attainment in schools of varying immigrant composition show that the attainment of children is affected by increasing concentrations of immigrant children only at the two tails of the frequency distribution. In other words, where immigrant pupils constitute less than 10% of the enrolment and where they constitute more than 60% of the school's enrolment, attainment levels are affected. Varying proportions in between 10% and 60% appear to make little difference to attainment levels.[16] For this and other reasons outlined above, most people are now inclined to the view that what matters is not the number or concentration of ethnic minority children in schools but what goes on within these schools.[17] It is the capacity of schools to organise themselves and to be able to obtain sufficient resources (experienced staff etc.) which is the crucial determinant of the educational adjustment of both ethnic minority and indigenous children.

Language Needs of Ethnic Minority Pupils
Another policy issue which was raised concerns the needs of ethnic minority children for language tuition within the education system. It was initially supposed that these children would 'pick up the language' from their English colleagues in schools. But the demonstration that ethnic minority pupils achieve lower levels of performance across the range of subjects in the curriculum indicated that a more structured approach to their language needs was required and that such language tuition facilities as are developed should include West Indian children who were initially not taken into account because they speak a form of the English language as against Asian children for whom English is a second language.

The recognition of this need and the fact that many local authorities provided language tuition facilities in the schools to which children were 'bussed' revealed a desperate shortage of skilled staff, teaching materials and, indeed, the virtual absence of teacher training courses which could have equipped teachers for careers in inner city schools which have sizeable proportions of ethnic minority pupils. The shortage continues to be felt today even though a number of training courses have now been instituted to deal with this problem. The Leeds Project under June Derrick, supported by the

Schools Council, produced teaching materials for pupils with inadequate English as well as course syllabi for children in junior schools. Many teachers in inner city schools have been associated with the Leeds Project. However, it is difficult to know the full extent of the coverage of inner city schools by such teachers since no general evaluation of the effect of this project has been published. A similar project was started at Birmingham University in 1967 under Professors Taylor and Sinclair to produce material for improving the language proficiency of West Indian children. This material is now widely available though it is difficult to assess its impact.

These developments were encouraged and supported by local authorities and by teachers; nevertheless, there is still a shortage of qualified teachers of English as a second language, which would require additional and direct financial support from central government as was done in 1967 under Section 11 of the Local Government Act 1966. Further, much more effort is required to evaluate the advantages and disadvantages (from a paedagogic point of view) of the various administrative arrangements which have been made for teaching immigrant children English. Such an evaluation would also help to demonstrate which arrangements are best suited to language training for infants — an area which has been even more neglected because of the belief among many infant teachers that specialised language teaching is not relevant to the socialization of infants, unlike their beliefs in the continuing re-inforcement of language in secondary schools.[18]

Achievement Patterns and ESN School Placement

The language needs of ethnic minority pupils have a direct link with their achievement patterns within schools as well as the question of their representation in ESN schools. Various surveys have shown that ethnic minority pupils tend to perform less well in school compared to their indigenous counterparts and there is a strong supposition that this is closely related to their language needs, their unfamiliarity with the culture of the school in the UK and the fact that they have not received all their previous education in the U.K. Townsend and Brittan interviewed Headmasters who expressed concern about the relatively low performance of ethnic minority pupils in junior and secondary schools compared to their indigenous counterparts; among ethnic minority groups as a whole, they expressed more concern about West Indian pupils than they did about Asians and Cypriots even though all ethnic minority group pupils performed less well than their indigenous colleagues.

One of the latest surveys[19] undertaken in 1971-72 with Pakistani and Indian pupils in Scottish schools showed that on average Pakistani pupils performed less well than Scottish children, had lower IQ scores and were at least six months behind in their reading standards (their sex being unrelated to their performance). The earlier survey of London school children to which reference was made earlier found that immigrant children as a group performed less well compared to the under-privileged indigenous children who are found in these schools.[20] These studies were all undertaken with children in primary schools in London. Another survey undertaken in Newcastle showed that Asian pupils achieved higher performance scores than their indigenous counterparts — a result which reflects on the different basis on which the samples were selected.[21] These studies demonstrate that there is cause for concern since these results reflect the extent to which the schools are meeting the educational needs of ethnic minority children as a whole.

It might well be that there are different factors in the background socialisation of ethnic minority pupils as against that of indigenous pupils which place them at a disadvantage in the education system. Further, these background factors do not apply only to those ethnic minority pupils who have been educated in the U.K. for only a short time, it probably also applies to those who have had ten years or more of their schooling in this country, thus suggesting that these background factors operate in the pre-school socialisation of these children rather than in the length of schooling which they have had in the country even though length of school does contribute to higher performance scores among ethnic minority children.

There are a number of factors within the school environment itself which could have contributed to these results: the influence of teacher's attitudes, the supportiveness or otherwise of parents, language difficulties, the lack of meaningfulness in school. However, no work has been done on the influence of these factors on the school achievement of immigrant pupils in the United Kingdom though there is a surfeit of information about these factors in the U.S.A. What is certain, however, is that the 'learning environment' within the school contributes, if not determines, the extent to which children under-perform.

It is their low performance as measured by standard school achievement tests and assessments which has contributed to the fact that higher proportions of ethnic minority pupils are ascertained as either being unqualified for jobs[22] or as being in need of special education in ESN schools compared to their indigenous counterparts; and of these, by far the majority are West Indian children.[23] However, the ascertainment and de-ascertainment procedures have been brought into question since fewer ethnic minority children compared to indigenous pupils are de-ascertained and can return to their normal schools. Besides, a number of Heads interviewed in the Townsend & Brittan survey expressed the view that there were significant proportions of children in ESN schools who should not have been there in terms of their ability. Clearly, while the relatively lower achievement levels of ethnic minority children makes it more likely that they would be over-represented in ESN schools, nevertheless there is need for a close and critical examination of the ascertainment and de-ascertainment procedures.

The debate about culture-free tests and the extent to which standard tests such as the IQ test can be applied to children who are unfamiliar with the cultural background of the society in which it is applied, has probably run its course and has resulted in attempts to develop culture-free tests.[24] In this regard, it has been suggested that the search for a culture-free test must remain a difficult one since education is, by its very nature, culture-based. If this is so, then ethnic minority pupils must be encouraged to achieve levels of performance in schools which are comparable to those of their indigenous colleagues and bears a statistical relationship, at least, to their representation in the schools. If the debate on culture-free tests has run its course, the debate on the ascertainment and de-ascertainment for ESN provision has barely begun. Only a critical scrutiny of the way these procedures have operated in the past would suffice to allay the anxieties of those parents of ethnic minority children who have perceived the operation of institutional racial discrimintion in the operation of ESN schools.[25]

Socio-economic Background and Pre-school Preparation

The above-mentioned evidence on the academic achievement of ethnic minority pupils in British schools suggests that the reasons for their low performance are to be found in the pre-school provision which ethnic minority parents make for their children. A medical study of ethnic minority and indigenous three-year olds in Brixton showed that the former are deprived in terms of a number of pre-school play opportunities and in terms of the degree of stimulation which they receive from their parents.[26] Other studies have, in fact, suggested that this is generalisable beyond the area in which Pollak undertook her investigation. This is in part a reflection of the socio-economic background of ethnic minority parents which restricts the extent to which they can provide such materials required by young children (toys) and of their heavy commitment to working long hours as we saw earlier, thus being unable to afford sufficient time for children.

It may, of course, be doubted whether the issue of pre-school socialisation and its role in preparing children for school is anything as simple as the mere physical possession of play materials may lead one to suppose, for the interaction between parent and child in the early years is so complex that while the differences which have been shown by studies such as Pollak's are undoubtedly valid, it is unlikely that they play a simple causal role in the deprivation of ethnic minority children during their pre-school years. Nevertheless, these differences do highlight the disadvantages which ethnic minority pupils experience during their pre-school years which lead over into their school years. These can, in fact, be handled by specific programmes of compensatory education (such as that undertaken in Dundee by the EPA Project) which can lead to an improvement in the test scores of these children.[27]

Ethnic Identity
A further important point of difference between ethnic minority children and their indigenous counterparts in the schools concerns the extent to which the cultural heritage and self-esteem of the indigenous child is re-inforced by the books he uses in school, by the teachers who teach him and by the fact that he lives in a society in which he is not a stranger nor of an identifiably different colour. The ethnic minority pupil is in a very different position: he receives very little re-inforcement of the cultural ideas of the society from which he or his parents emigrated, will invariably be taught by indigenous teachers and would, in fact, use books and other materials which relate to British society rather than to the society from which he derived. In addition, he is of an identifiable colour and would have experienced racial discrimination in the society in some connection or another. All these factors are likely to affect his adjustment to the school situation. This is a point of difference between the ethnic minority child and his indigenous colleague, whose significance has not yet been grasped. It is in this connection that Black Studies have been thought of as having a major role to play; however, many teachers are opposed to Black Studies because they see a reverse of racial discrimination in the suggestion (What about White Studies?''); consequently, little effort has been put into developing a generally acceptable curriculum.[28]

However, a number of studies have shown some of the consequences which can arise if a sense of worth is not cultivated in children by the education system. Christopher Bagley and Bernard Coard showed, in their study of black children in three London Schools, that these children reject their black skins, are contemptuous of themselves, are ignorant of significant heroes from the societies from which they and their parents emigrated and so on[29]; they are also more likely to be described as exhibiting 'behaviour problems' in schools. Very much the same range of traits was found by other investigators such as Milner in 1971 who presented 400 English, West Indian, Pakistani and Indian children (aged 5 to 8) with dolls with which they were to identify themselves on a 'like me' basis. He found that whereas 76% of Asian and all the English children correctly identified the correct colours of the dolls, only 52% of West Indian children did so.[30] This is in contrast to studies of self-esteem among black children in the United States a decade ago and today[31] which show a dramatic improvement in their levels of self-esteem.

It may be argued, to be sure, that just as ethnic minority children should adjust to the circumstances and tests that apply in schools because the United Kingdom is their home, that this evidence of self-rejection is of little consequence. However, since 'behaviour problems' have in fact been one of those problems which characterise West Indian pupils in schools, the possible contribution of a lack of self-esteem to such behaviour cannot be overlooked quite apart from the positive contributions to achievement in schools which a congenial sense of worth can make.

Survey Findings on Education
While the five issues we have outlined above have been significant in policy thinking on a national level, they have not all been equally significant in every local education authority area; and even when some of them were significant, the degree of significance attributed to them varied according to the immigrant composition of the area. For example, the issue of 'bussing' was always a significant issue on a national level but was not significant in every local education authority area because some authorities did not implement the principle of dispersal by 'bussing' which was recommended in Circular 7/65 to which we referred earlier.

Our surveys of 'decision-makers', professional practitioners and laymen were designed to capture the views of our respondents on those issues which impinged either on their lives or on their role as parents of school-children involved in these issues or on their role as policy 'decision-makers'; they were also designed to find out the extent to which the different 'levels' of respondents were aware of the extent to which educational needs have been met in urban areas and to find out the views of immigrant parents about their children's education. Accordingly, our surveys focused on the following issues: the issue of concentration and 'bussing', the implications of the reported under-achievement of immigrant pupils in schools for contact between the Home and the School, the issue of curriculum changes which would enable immigrant children to identify themselves more with the curriculum (e.g. curriculum changes to reflect the different cultural backgrounds of immigrant children including the issue of instruction in the mother tongue and single sex schools for girls) and the issue of the availability and desirability of immigrant staff in schools with immigrant pupils in inner city areas.

Concentrations in Schools — 'Decision-makers'
It will be recalled that the policy of dispersal of immigrant children which was announced in 1965 was partly influenced by political considerations and partly by educational ones. Since the policy has provided the overall framework within which local authorities have operated over the past decade, we were concerned to find out the extent to which 'decision-makers' feel that it is still justified as a means of dealing with concentrations in inner city areas, the extent to which they see the issue of concentration itself as still having either educational or political implications irrespective of the mechanisms by which it

is dealt with; in this regard, we were interested to find out the extent to which the considerations that precluded some authorities from adopting dispersal from the very beginning, in the case of those who did not follow it up, still remain valid.

As a point of departure, we asked 'decision-makers': "Do you feel that concentrations of any category of children in schools is an issue of significance?" The responses emphasised educational problems in the main:

"it is an issue of significance. It is a constraint potentially though not necessarily a bad one since it introduces a factor which is not present in every school or college. And the minute you get that, I don't think you can assume that you have the same conditions you might have in an institution with children from a completely similar ethnic and social background. The teachers themselves become stereotyped if they are teaching all lower or all higher ability children. I also think that it is essential in a multi-racial society that English children should have the opportunity of growing up alongside children of immigrant parentage."

"Concentration is an issue of significance because there may well be children with problems who may be missed in the crowd."

However, there was one exceptional response which turned on the political implications of concentrations of ethnic minority children in inner city schools. This respondent said:

"I think it is an issue of signficiance insofar as it is perceived by a lot of people to be an issue of signficiance. In a society in which there was less racial discrimination, in which people did not see the presence of ethnic minority children as odd, it would not be an issue of significance over and above the concentration of any category of white children. But it is seen as an issue of significance not only by the host population but also by the more aspirant members of minority groups who themselves object to what they feel may be ghetto schools."

Nevertheless, those that operated a system of dispersal justified it in terms of its practical advantages in dealing with spare school places in outer city schools, the past difficulty of obtaining funds to build more schools in inner city areas or to re-furbish outdated ones, the need to disperse children to schools with adequate language facilities and the need to ensure that children with problems are channelled to outer city schools with resources to handle these problems — all of them basically educational reasons rather than political ones. Equally, authorities who never adopted 'bussing' initially justified their action in terms of educational reasons.

However, those who initially adopted dispersal by 'bussing', but subsequently decided to abandon it, justified their decision in terms of the administrative and other costs involved in operating a 'bussing' scheme for large numbers of children but still felt that concentrations of ethnic minority children in inner city schools have educational implications and that 'bussing' was a useful way of dealing with them but not the only way.

In sum, most of the respondents felt that concentrations of ethnic minority pupils in inner city schools remain an issue of some educational significance which will have to be dealt with in the future by mechanisms other than by 'bussing' — i.e. additional input of resources into inner city schools, more school buildings in these areas and other methods of positive discrimination in favour of these areas.

In order to clarify these issues further, we explored the extent to which our respondents viewed the concentration of ethnic minority children differently from the concentration of other categories of children (e.g. lower ability, special problems etc.). The responses showed that the presence of immigrants in inner city schools has affected policies insofar as it has called for additional resources (e.g. staff who are trained in the cultural background of these children) which would not have been necessary if the entire school population in these areas consisted of indigenous children:

> "Six years ago, if there hadn't been immigrant children we would have abolished all large classes. I'm not blaming immigrants for that but stating a fact. Now we are going to have to start bussing because of the lack of school places."

> "Personally, we would rather have 100% immigrant schools and use the concentration to improve the resources of the school but we are not allowed."

It may have been supposed from these responses that our 'decision-makers' would have welcomed such positive discrimination measures such as the ESP payments to teachers which resulted from the EPA projects, Urban Aid and Section 11 grants. In fact, while they appreciated the principle of positive discrimination to inner urban areas implicit in these grants, they were critical of the administrative arrangements which are employed to give effect to the principle:

> "The Urban Aid Programme is a waste of money. It's useless to hand funds in penny packets. If the government is serious about urban deprivation, then they've got to identify the degree of seriousness of the problem and give massive support. The 25% formula (i.e. local authority's guaranteed contribution) is useless; councils have to control expenditure and often find it difficult to raise their contribution."

> "We strongly deplore the way the EPA was brought about. We would rather have the money to employ more teachers rather than give this money to those who work in particular schools. It doesn't make them

better teachers paying them £270 more. They don't do any more work. They may stay a little longer but those who do are the ones who are really engaged on the work anyway. It's early days yet; but in five years time you will find that all the EPA teachers are those who could not get better jobs elsewhere.''

Home/School Contact

All our respondents suggested that Home/School contact among parents of ethnic minority children was very inadequate and that this may be an important contribution to the reported under-achievement of ethnic minority children compared to indigenous ones. One respondent, however, sounded a note of caution when he said:

"I think there is a danger in making too clear a distinction between immigrant children and their indigenous counterparts in terms of their relative achievement and performance levels. I think the immigrant youngster whose family backs him in his schooling, gives full support to the school does achieve as much as his indigenous counterpart just as an indigenous family who gives no support to the youngster can lead to the boy doing badly in school. I think there is a danger in making too synonymous 'immigrants' and 'under-achievers'. Many of our immigrant pupils achieve a lot through the education system. Where they don't it is often for the same reasons as English children — lack of contact with the school on the part of the parents. There is a real danger in presuming that immigrants as a group under-achieve in our schools. They don't."

Those respondents from authorities with Immigrant Education Centres tried to involve immigrant parents in their children's education by involving them in the activities of these centres. All respondents reported that the level of participation in PTA's by ethnic minority parents is inadequate; when these parents are involved, they are less likely to be the parents whose participation is more desirable (i.e. working class parents); it is most often the middle class parent who participates and maintains contact with the school.

They therefore suggested that future improvement can be expected only if (a) the mystic of the school is reduced in the minds of these parents (b) they are involved in the activities of the school other than for reasons connected with their children's education e.g. adult language classes for Asians in school premises and (c) more staff are appointed with a responsibility for making contact with parents in their own homes in the evenings. All our respondents reported that some such staff have been appointed in their area (Home/School Visitor, teacher/social workers, education support teams) but that their numbers are below what is required.

Curriculum Changes to Reflect the Cultural Background of Pupils in Schools

It has often been suggested that ethnic minority children would respond more positively to the education system than they have done in the past and perform better if the curriculum of the school was itself more responsive to their cultural backgrounds because the degree of alienation which exists between these children and the schools would be reduced. A number of changes have been suggested which would have this effect, the most significant of which are:

1. Courses on the cultural background of children in inner city schools.
2. Instruction in the mother-tongue of these children at least in the early stages of their education.
3. The establishment and/or expansion of single sex schools for girls and
4. The appointment of teaching staff drawn from ethnic minority groups with whom ethnic minority children would identify and thus bolster up their sense of identity.

In the course of our survey, we explored the views of 'decision-makers' on these issues.

All our respondents recognised the need for teachers with a knowledge of the cultural background of ethnic minority children but were in the main opposed to the establishment of special courses in schools or the appointment of ethnic minority staff, and the establishment or expansion of single sex schools for girls in an age when the thrust of demand for education is for mixed co-educational schools:

"I am against black studies. If you select one aspect of the curriculum like that you set up a reaction among white kids. I believe in a balanced curriculum using an indirect approach to race relations. You'll get a racially just society if you provide all children with sufficient educational resources."

"Mother tongue instruction is a problem for the community, not for the school. We have had requests for Gujerati and Urdu to be taught in schools but we are against it. If they live and work here, their first need is to speak and write English. If we taught mother-tongue in schools, we would have thirty or forty languages in some schools. If ethnic minorities want their languages taught at week-ends, that's fine."

"Fifteen years ago, this problem was relevant. Now, the majority of children in schools were born here and any attempt to talk about background cultures would drive divisions among the children."

"Learning the cultural background of your family is important but this is not the job of the school; it is the responsibility of the home."

"If they are going to live and make their future in this country they should conform. I personally do not see it as the job of our schools to cater for other traditions and cultures. If they wish to keep their cultures around them, they can do it privately. The Jews have always maintained their own religion and instruction in Hebrew privately. I do not see this as a problem."

"We have no policy of employing certain teachers of immigrants in schools. I am very much against any attempt to direct immigrant teachers to these schools because this has the implication that you don't think that they are fit enough to teach anybody else; one has to be very careful about that. Further, I also think that people should have the right to choose; if you are an Asian and you don't want to teach in a school with many Asian kids, then I think that's great."

Overall, the feeling was that teacher training has not prepared existing staff to handle the problems which the presence of ethnic minority pupils give rise to and that improvement in this aspect of their training would equip all teachers for work in inner city schools. Since some of these teachers are themselves likely to be drawn from the ethnic minority groups, the advantage of their being seen to be in positions of authority would be secured. However, it was felt that it would be unwise to appoint ethnic minority teachers for ethnic minority pupils in inner city areas.

Laymen's Interview Findings
In order to round out our exploration of the policy issues in education, we also interviewed a total of 1,403 laymen (ethnic minority and indigenous people) living in inner city areas and raised basically the same set of questions; however, these questions were directed at their role as parents of immigrant pupils in inner city schools.

In this connection, we explored their knowledge and understanding of the education which their children was receiving. This also enabled us to explore their own perceptions of the education system. Accordingly, we expected them to either be unaware of some of the policy issues which 'decision-makers' have raised or be unable to articulate them in terms of their wider educational and/or political implications. We therefore focused our range of questions on those aspects of their children's education with which they are likely to be familiar (e.g. do your children go to the nearest school? Did you decide to send them to schools which are farther away from home or was the decision taken by the Local Authority?) These findings do not therefore constitute a direct test of the extent to which the issues raised by policy-makers impinge on the lives of their children nor do they necessarily indicate a gulf between the views of policy-makers and the parents as 'consumers' of education. Nevertheless, they do provide an indirect indication of the extent to which parents are satisfied that the education system is meeting the needs of their children.

Satisfaction with Children's Education

Respondents were asked for their opinions about the schools which their children attend. The findings showed that 47% of them either had no complaints or could not think of anything they disliked about these schools. On the other hand, only 10% of the sample positively approved of the schools as being very good. Of those who positively approved, there was a systematic breakdown between various groups with West Indians and Cypriots being the least likely to do so and Urdu speakers being more likely to do so.

Those who disliked the schools their children attend mentioned a number of reasons for this. Firstly, Sikhs, Urdu and Punjabi speakers in one project area felt that the schools which their children attended were too far away from their homes. Indeed, just over one-third of all respondents with children in their households over the age of five went to schools other than those which are nearest to their homes. When the reasons for this were examined, it was found that parental choice was more influential in the case of White British and West Indian parents as against Asian parents whose choice was constrained by the local education authority. Understandably, the proportions of parents reporting that their children went to schools other than those nearest to their homes varied with project areas as Table 13 shows.

TABLE 13: Children Not Going to Nearest School (Ethnics & Whites)

Project Areas	1 %	2 %	3 %	4 %	5 %	6 %	7 %	8 %	All %
Any child not going to nearest school	58	29	26	36	29	41	42	43	37

Secondly, a number of respondents felt that little instruction was given in their religious and cultural backgrounds in schools; nor was instruction given in their mother-tongues. But within ethnic minority groups as a whole some one in four Indian, Pakistani and East African Asian respondents gave this response (respectively). Basically, the same pattern of responses was obtained when respondents were broken down into language groups. 47% of Gujerati speakers felt that instruction should be given in their own language in schools as against 27% of Urdu, Hindi and Punjabi speakers. Cypriots were the least likely to give this response to the question of instruction in their mother tongue.

Thirdly, one respondent in four considered that the discipline in the schools attended by their children is inadequate; 2% claimed that it is too strict, 12% felt that it is not strict enough and a further 11% felt that it was virtually non-existent.

These reasons are largely based on respondents' perceptions as to the kind of education which they would like their children to have as distinct from that which they are actually having. In order to examine their views on the education that their children are actually having, we asked them whether they feel that their children are either having or have had problems in school as a direct or indirect result of being ethnic minority pupils. The responses obtained were interesting not only in terms of the range of problems which were highlighted but also in terms of the distribution among ethnic groups of those who felt that their children are having and have had problems because of their being ethnic minority pupils. Overall, 82% reported that their children have not had problems on this score. But among all ethnic minority groups, Cypriots are the least likely to report that their children have had problems deriving from the fact of their being ethnic minority pupils; the other groups were equally likely to report problems on this score. When ethnic groups were examined in terms of religion, the Sikhs were the least likely to report that their children have had problems stemming from this source.

When the problems were examined, a range of problems emerged, as in Table 14, with bullying coming out at the top of the list of problems mentioned.

TABLE 14: Problems of Ethnic Minority Pupils*

	%
Bullying by other children	42
Teachers unhelpful	19
There is race prejudice	18
Language Problems	15

*This table excludes reponses made by less than 5% of respondents.

Of the small minority who thought that their children experienced problems in schools because they were ethnic minority pupils, one in three thought that the school did not try to solve these problems; yet some 57% of such parents did not visit the school in order to discuss these problems with their children's teachers — thus highlighting the inadequacy of home/school contact which the 'decision-makers' stressed.

Since the declared raison d'etre of the dispersal policy announced in Circular 7/65 was the need to ensure that ethnic minority pupils who need extra language instruction get it and since, as we have seen, sizeable proportions of ethnic minority pupils have been involved in dispersal (schools other than those nearest to their homes), it may be supposed that pupils with language problems would have been involved in special language instruction. Our findings show that only 10% of these parents had children who had received special instruction in English. Those whose children had attended classes for English language instruction were asked how useful they thought it had been for them. Just over half (57%) thought that it had been very useful since the children learned to speak English properly. 18% thought that it had been a waste of time. When those whose children had not been involved in language instruction classes were asked whether it would have been helpful for their children if they had done so, 49% said that it was not necessary but 40% felt that it would have been helpful, with West Indian and Cypriot parents being less likely to feel that it would have been helpful to their children. Taking these results together then, some 40% of parents felt that special language instruction would have been helpful to their children but only 10% reported that their children had received such instruction.

Finally, we inquired into the issue of teaching staff drawn from ethnic minority groups. Only one in seven West Indian parents said that there was a West Indian teacher in their children's school; Cypriot and Indian Asians were more likely to have teachers from their own cultural background teaching their children. Respondents whose children do not have teachers from their own ethnic background were asked whether they would have liked them. West Indians were equally divided on this question but some three-quarters each of Cypriots and Asians would have liked them, with Asians justifying this feeling in terms of having someone who understands their children's background culture, religion and language. West Indian parents wanting West Indian teachers were most likely to hold the view that there is better understanding between people of the same race, with only a very small minority mentioning the advantage of teaching their culture to their children. The majority of those who did not want teachers from their own country or ethnic group felt that there was no particular advantage to be gained from it: "it doesn't matter so long as they are trained". A further 11% felt that their children are English and should therefore be taught by English teachers.

Summary

Our discussion in this chapter has been focused on policy issues which have arisen in the field of education and which remain pertinent to the education of ethnic minority and indigenous children in inner city schools. We showed that their concentration is still an issue of significance among decision-makers and 'bussing' is disliked by the parents because it takes the children to schools which are considered to be far away from their homes. We also showed that contact between the home and the school is not only considered to be inadequate by the 'decision-makers' but was clearly shown to be so in the case of those parents who reported that their children had difficulties in school but did not visit the school to discuss these problems with teachers. Among 'decision-makers', there was a clear opposition to changes in the curriculum in the direction of providing instruction in mother tongues, black studies, single sex schools and the appointment of ethnic minority staff as a special consideration in relation to the education of ethnic minority children. This is in contrast to the wishes of the parents who are in favour of studies dealing with their cultural, and religious backgrounds and instruction in their mother tongues; they felt that teachers who share their cultural background are not only more likely to be able to provide these kinds of instruction but would also be able to 'understand' the children better. In sum, most parents of ethnic minority children were relatively satisfied (47%) with the education of their children but only 10% positively approved of the schools which their children attend largely because of their criticism of the above-mentioned aspects of these schools.

Chapter Five: Youth Service Provision for Ethnic Minority and Indigenous Youth

If the Education Act 1944 imposed a general obligation on local education authorities to provide education for all those children who require it, it also imposed a statutory obligation on those authorities to make general provision for young people by empowering them (Sec. 53) to secure full-time and part-time further education facilities for those over the compulsory school leaving age of 14 years. The compulsory school leaving age has now been raised to 16 (in 1972) and the age of majority has been reduced to 18. Nevertheless, the statutory age limits for those entitled to such facilities as are provided by local education authorities remain 14 to 20-year-olds. The suggestion has been made by the Fairbairn and Milson sub-committees of the Youth Service Development Council (in their report *Youth and Community Work in the 70s*) that these age limits should be abolished partly because they do not reflect sociological changes which have taken place among young people — earlier marriage among girls, a much enlarged commercial provision for young people such as discotheques and sports clubs etc — and partly because they contribute to the questionable conception of youth work as something separate and distinct from the rest of the community at large.

Nevertheless, local education authorities are obliged by statute to cater for the needs of young people between the ages of 14 and 20 in partnership with voluntary bodies. Our investigation of youth provision and the disadvantages which ethnic minorities experience in this connection was undertaken within the context of this statutory obligation even though voluntary organisations, especially the uniformed ones (Girl Guides, Boy Scouts etc.) have played an important part in meeting the needs of young people in general.

Objective of the Youth Service
The formal objective of the Youth Service can be defined in the words of Sir John Maude as:
> "To offer individual young people in their leisure time opportunities of various kinds, complementary to those of home, formal education and work, to discover and develop their personal resources of body, mind and spirit and thus the better equip themselves to live the life of mature, creative and responsible member of a free society."[1]

However, this objective has been variously interpreted in various areas by various voluntary bodies (Church organisations, uniformed organisations) in ways which are more directly relevant to their ideologies, locality and the characteristics of the young people in their areas.

However, and in spite of these variations, youth provision by voluntary and statutory bodies is based on the assumption that a small group fosters the adolescent's personality because it provides him with a community of his own which is different from other communities to which he is forced to belong e.g. family groups, work groups and school groups. By meeting other young people in a free atmosphere, unrestrained by the rules which normally apply in other groups, it is assumed that the adolescent will discover his own creative potential and, at the same time, direct his energies away from anti-social and delinquent pursuits into more creative channels. In this way, he will learn to occupy his role in the wider community and be enabled to feel a part and parcel of it.

Not only do these assumptions remain valid today, but they have been brought into sharp relief as reports about the criminality and delinquency of young people in general, and ethnic minority adolescents in particular, increase. Reports about 'mugging' merely reflect a sensational approach to what is an important issue of concern in modern society.

It is against this background that the disadvantages which ethnic minority adolescents have experienced in the area of youth provision can be displayed. This is best done by considering the statistical patterns of demand for youth facilities among ethnic minority and indigenous adolescents on the basis of information available in the 1971 Census and by looking at some of the qualitative issues which influence the appeal of youth facilities provided by statutory and voluntary bodies. We shall then go on to discuss the results of our survey of young people, youth workers and 'decision-makers' which formed an integral part of this project.

Statistical Patterns

The demand for youth facilities is, in part, a function of the proportions of adolescents in the country who are between the ages of 14 and 20 years. However, there are major disparities between the proportions of indigenous adolescents in this age group and those of ethnic minority communities which influence their relative 'need' for youth facilities quite apart from the question as to whether this need is adequately met. Census information is not classified according to the statutory age limits of 14 to 20 year olds, nevertheless it provides a rough indication of the relative proportions of both groups of adolescents to whom existing youth facilities should appeal all things being equal. It shows that while all ethnic minority people from the New Commonwealth consitute 2.1% of the total population of Great Britain, their children constitute 3.0% of all those in the total population who are between the ages of 11-20 years.

Their over-representation in this age group is brought into even sharper relief if we consider the relative proportions of those whose parents were born in the New Commonwealth and in the United Kingdom (i.e. excluding those whose parents were born in the Old Commonwealth, the Irish Republic and foreign countries). In this case, whereas those of New Commonwealth-born parentage constitute only 2.1% of the UK population in the country, their children constitute 5.6% of those between the ages of 11 and 20 years of age. In other words, their children are almost three times more likely to fall within this group compared to those of UK parentage. This can be presented in another way: whereas indigenous 11-20 years olds constitute only 8.2% of the population of the UK, ethnic minority 11-20 year olds constitute 20.2%. The logic of these figures would suggest that three adolescents from ethnic minority groups should be making use of youth facilities for every one indigenous youth who does so, all things being equal. This, in point of fact, is not the case; all things are not equal.

An extensive survey[2] of youth service provision undertaken for the Department of Education and Science in 1972 showed that the overall use of such youth club facilities as exist is confined to no more than 26% of all those who are between the ages of 14 and 20 years,[3] but that within this pattern of use, there is a significant tendency for the use of youth facilities to decline between the ages of 17 and 20; indeed, the 14 to 16 year olds consistently use these facilities more than those who are between 17 and 20 years of age. Taking this statistical pattern of use into account, it is easy to see that more adolescents of New Commonwealth parentage are likely to fall into those groups which are less inclined to use youth club facilities. Table 15 presents a breakdown of Census figures into those who are younger than 16 and those who are older. Though the preponderance of New Commonwealth adolescents is evident in both age groups, a larger proportion (10.9%) of them fall into the 16-20 year group and are therefore less likely to use youth club facilities, all things being equal.

TABLE 15: Age Breakdown and Comparison of New Commonwealth and Indigenous Adolescents

	11-15 years %	16-20 years %
U.K. Adolescents	7.6	6.8
New Commonwealth	9.4	10.9

Source: *Census* 1971, p.103 Table 2.

101

The proportion of those who require such facilities and who are statistically speaking, more likely to use them is still large (9.4%) nevertheless. But do they use them? Is there a higher use of these facilities by ethnic minority adolescents aged 11-15 years than by indigenous adolescents as their representation in this age category would lead one to expect?

It is difficult to give an unequivocal answer to this question partly because this kind of data is not available and partly because the major survey undertaken by Margaret Bone did not single out ethnic minority adolescents as a special category for consideration. Nevertheless, the indications that are available from the few surveys that have been undertaken in various localities would seem to suggest that fewer ethnic minority adolescents are involved in youth facilities than their statistical representation in the age categories of 14-20 years would lead one to expect. For example, Eric Butterworth's survey of youth provision in Bradford in 1966 showed that there were relatively few adolescents from ethnic minorities who were involved in youth club activities in that city in spite of the fact that Bradford had (and still has) a sizeable proportion of ethnic minorities. The few that were members were regular in their attendance and joined in club activities in the same way as other members. He concluded that little attempt had been made to involve young people from ethnic minority communities in youth club provision. Other surveys have come to more or less the same conclusion even though they were, like Butterworth's survey, based on local areas.[4]

Nevertheless, our discussion of the statistical modalities pertaining to indigenous and ethnic minority adolescents would seem to suggest not only a considerably low level of use of youth facilities by all adolescents but would also seem to suggest that ethnic minority adolescents use these facilities much less than their statistical representation would lead one to expect. Clearly, the youth service does not have much of an appeal for most adolescents today; but beyond that, it has failed to appeal to adolescents from ethnic minority groups. Why?

A number of reasons have been advanced by experienced field-workers; little research has been undertaken into this whole issue though Margaret Bone's work did much to provide hard data for all adolescents in an area in which speculation was rife.

One reason which has been advanced concerns the nature of the immigrant communities themselves and their cultural patterns of control over their adolescent chidren. Asian groups are not only strict about the participation of girls in mixed activities, but also have dietary and other restrictions which apply to boys as well as to girls. Such restrictions influence social intercourse with other groups. Further, the strong tradition of family solidarity within the Asian family has disposed Asian adolescents to seek their leisure pursuits from within their own circles even where their fluency in the English language is such that they could well utilise the facilities which are locally provided for all young people. West Indians also maintain strong discipline especially over the activities of girls and the hours they spend away from home even though they are less inclined to object to their daughters attending mixed youth clubs. It is significant that where reports of increased recruitment of ethnic minorities by youth organisations have been made, they have concerned international and/or uniformed organisations such as the Junior Red Cross, Boy Scouts, Girl Guides, Boys Brigade and church groups and have involved primarily West Indian youth as against other groups of ethnic minorities. Indeed, all the available reports would seem to suggest that if ethnic minority adolescents are using youth facilities, it is these organisations which have been more successful in appealing to them as against the local youth services. This is partly because their parents would have been already familiar with these organisations before arriving in England and partly because of the appeal of the uniforms and the ideologies of these organisations; the fact that youth organisations connected with churches have been successful in recruiting West Indian adolescents reflects the fact that many West Indian parents form part of their congregations. This link between ethnic minority parents and youth organisations is absent in the case of Asian parents, quite apart from the other problems relating to cultural restrictions which are highlighted above.

A second explanation concerns the pattern of social selection which appears to be associated with a strong attachment to youth clubs. Margaret Bone analysed the characteristics of those adolescents who are attached to youth clubs and compared them to those characteristics of adolescents who are not attached to these clubs. Her results showed a clearly consistent pattern of social selectivity in operation. She found that those adolescents who are attached to youth clubs are invariably (a) between the ages of 14 and 16 (b) are less likely to contemplate leaving school at the compulsory school leaving age (c) are in full-time education (d) are more likely to use youth facilities provided in an educational establishment rather than in a place of employment or, indeed, away from educational establishments (e) are more likely to be boys rather than girls and (f) are less likely to have come from a working class background.

If these characteristics apply to adolescents from ethnic minorities as well as to their indigenous counterparts, then such adolescents who fall within these groups are likely to be attached to youth clubs. We have already demonstrated in an earlier chapter that ethnic minorities are concentrated in the lower rungs of the occupational hierarchy and are therefore likely to be working class.

The special situation pertaining to the restrictions on the activities of girls among Asians and West Indians take on a special meaning within this context even though they are cultural in origin. The marked tendency for ethnic minority adolescents to stay on in school beyond the school-leaving age has been widely commented upon and would seem to suggest, in terms of the above characteristics, that these adolescents would be more inclined to join youth club activities. On the other hand, we have seen that a not insignificant proportion of ethnic minority adolescents are older than 16 years of age (10.9%) and therefore fall into those age groups who are less likely to be attached to youth clubs. In terms of the social characteristics outlined by Margaret Bone therefore, the pattern of social selectivity which characterises those who are attached to youth clubs is likely to be common to ethnic minority adolescents. They are therefore likely to be uninterested in youth club facilities to the extent that they are older than 16 years of age and/or are girls.

A third explanation for the fact that adolescents from minority groups have not used the youth service as much as their numbers would have led one to expect concerns their changing demographic characteristics before 1966 and between 1966 and 1971. Before 1966, the proportions of ethnic minority adolescents falling into the 14 to 20 year old group was smaller than it has become since. According to the estimate in the Hunt Report (p.3), they constituted some 2% of those who were between 14 and 20 years of age in 1966. Even though their regional distribution throughout the country followed that of their parents, it was not thought worthwhile to specifically focus on their need or indeed, on the needs of any particular category of adolescents at that time in view of their small numbers.

Their small numbers apart, discussions about youth provision in this country since the end of the Second World War were concerned more with building up a viable youth service structure than with providing such content or programmes as would appeal to all young people or those with special requirements. Accordingly, the Albermarle Report had much to say about the 'bricks and mortar' aspects of youth provision — buildings, training facilities and expenditure for this purpose — but little to say about the content of programmes or indeed their appeal to different categories of young people. Not until the Hunt Report examined the question of immigrants and the youth service in 1967 did their participation become an issue of some significance for policy. In other words, the Youth service had not specifically considered its own appeal to young people in general and to ethnic minority adolescents in particular before 1967 on the one hand and ethnic minority adolescents, on the other, did not feel themselves part of the general community partly because they were few in numbers and partly because their existence did not, at that time, appear to carry serious implications for policy. We have seen, in fact, that ethnic minority children did not pose practical problems for educational policy before 1966 for largely the same reasons. The proportion of 14 to 20 year olds has increased to 3%; yet their very existence has now become a matter of some concern to policy-makers following the publication of the Hunt Report and the Circular (8/67) which was issued after its publication by the Minister of Education and Science.

These are undoubtedly three contributory factors for the fact that ethnic minority adolescents have not used the youth service as their statistical representation would have led one to expect. We suspected, at the beginning of this inquiry, that while these reasons may have been important in the past, it is matters concerning the content and style of presentation of youth programmes which are more crucial in determining the patterns of use of youth facilities today, a factor which the Keele University Project examined.[5] The Fairbain and Milson sub-committees of the Youth Service Development Council *(Youth and Community Work in the 70s)* were quite explicit in stressing the importance of appealing to the particular and special interests of young people when they said:

"It (i.e. the Youth Service i the 70s) should take account of the peculiar needs of particular social groups and individuals whether they be handicapped in any way or have specialist interests; and it should also take account of the development tasks of the young adult in our society, tasks which have to do with work and marriage and status.[6]

The questions which arose from this consideration and which were significant for our surveys were: Are the activities of youth clubs such that they would appeal to the interests of Asian, West Indian and Cypriot youngsters? Are they *presented* by youth leaders who are sympathetic to those interests and in a way which would appeal to their need for a feeling of security in a society in which they may have experienced racial discrimination and rejection in various spheres such as housing and employment? Can the appeal of youth clubs for ethnic minority adolescents and their internal activities be divorced from the actual or perceived rejection which they and their parents may have experienced in the wider society? Is the emphasis on the multi-racial presentation of youth clubs (as in the Hunt Report) likely to enhance their appeal to these adolescents or must 'integration' be a strait-jacket into which youth club provision must fit in spite of other considerations pertaining to local areas and to particular groups (such as Asian girls)?

Findings of the Youth Surveys

It was in order to clarify these issues that we included a sub-sample of young people in our study of ethnic minorities in urban areas and interviewed (a) adolescents between the ages of 16 and 20 from indigenous and ethnic minority communities in the eight project areas in which we carried out the project (b) youth workers — both club-based and detached, drawn from ethnic minority and the indigenous communities and (c) policy 'decision-makers' within the local authorities who are responsible for determining policy in connection with youth provision under the Education Act 1944.

Policy Objectives of Youth Provision

As a point of departure for our survey, we explored the policy objectives of local authority youth provision with the 'decision-makers' in the eight project areas and discussed some of the difficulties which they have experienced in implementing them. We asked them "What would you say are the overall objectives of your youth policy?"

There was considerable consensus about the broad objectives of youth provision. One respondent summarised these objectives by saying:

"To provide social education and to help adolescents develop into reasonably mature young people."

Another respondent described these objectives with particular stress on the 'out of school context' when he said:

"To provide young people in their particular adolescent period and in the *out of school context* with the opportunity of testing out the norms, the customs and the guidelines that they have absorbed in their families, home, school and community and to determine for themselves how far these norms are such that they are prepared to either adopt them as they stand or adopt them in a modified form."

However, while agreeing with the broad overall objectives of youth provision, this respondent was alone in stressing the 'out of school' context as the period which is relevant to the youth service. Every other respondent deplored the break between full-time education up to the age of 16 and the period between 16 and 21 and felt that the stability of school affiliation is often shattered when the adolescent leaves school; youth provision after that age should attempt to provide a similarly stable set of relationships for him but often fails for a variety of reasons, some of them having to do with the competition from commercial entertainment for adolescents' attentions.

In other words, they felt that youth provision should be more closely related to the period of full-time education than it is at the moment and therefore endorsed the establishment of youth centres in schools as the focus of youth provision. All respondents saw these policy objectives as applying to all adolescents irrespective of their ethnic or racial backgrounds; and a number of those who felt the need for closer co-ordination between provision in full-time education and youth provision after the school leaving age, stressed that they had been successful in invoking the interests of ethnic minority adolescents in this way. Further, ethnic minority parents of these adolescents have invariably approved of youth activities which take place after school hours but within the premises of the school and under the 'pastoral care' of teachers.

However, all of them felt that ethnic minority youths who are older than the school leaving age may not have been as actively provided for in terms of youth facilities and that it is in this respect that ethnic minority youths call for special consideration. None of them felt that the existence of ethnic minority adolescents in the areas for which they are responsible posed special issues for the policy objectives of their departments; on the contrary, the policy objectives should apply to all adolescents irrespective of their race, class or ethnic background. The issue as to how to involve ethnic minority adolescents in youth club provision after the school leaving age was seen as a largely practical one which required practical solutions.

In expanding on this point, all respondents felt that a very flexible approach is the best way to achieve the above-stated policy objectives, with practical solutions being adopted for particular groups in their areas. However, it was not felt that such groups should be defined in terms of their cultural or racial background but that such groups should be defined by their interests. These interests may be circumscribed by cultural values e.g. Asian girls, Polish and Ukrainian groups, Welsh Presbyterian and Scottish country dancing groups, but are not always determined by such values. It was in this particular connection that the sensitivity to which we referred earlier emerged for it was clear that a number of 'decision-makers' are unwilling to pursue the logical implications of their attachment to a flexible approach to the point where youth provision for particular ethnic groups is provided.

One respondent brought this out clearly when he said that no special issues of policy are raised by the existence of ethnic minority adolescents in his area and declared that his council would not look favourably on the idea of special consideration for particular ethnic groups and, if even it did, "would not know where to begin" and added that "here's an area where we ought to be working something". He expanded on this by discussing the dilemma which his colleagues had experienced on this issue when he said:

"If one starts providing professionally separate expertise, one creates separateness. Once you start providing something extra for one section of the community no matter what it is, the other people on the other side, whether they are in the majority or in the minority, think that they are getting something extra; and in so doing you build up barriers."

In other words, 'decision-makers' viewed the objectives of their departments in an objective way and were unwilling to allow issues concerning special needs to influence those objectives. Where special needs were considered, they were viewed in terms of interest groups rather than in terms of ethnic groups, the broad implication being that the interests of ethnic minority adolescents cut across the general spectrum of interests of all adolescents (e.g. hi-fi groups, sports clubs, etc). The problem of providing facilities which would appeal to the interests of the ethnic minority adolescents as stressed by the Hunt Report was therefore viewed in terms involving them in existing provision for a wide range of interests rather than in terms of providing separate facilities. Their involvement was therefore viewed as a practical matter which requires practical solutions.

One respondent stressed the practical solution which he adopted to a particular problem when he said:

> "About ... years ago, there was a definite policy. We felt at that time that ethnic groups should not be encouraged to feature separately in youth provision ... But it soon became obvious to me that this was not practical and the work did not develop beyond that. It was obvious that the Asian girl could not be expected to make use of existing provision and that something separate had to be set up, and this was done — an Asian girl's club ... It is not a case of opening the doors and saying 'We are meeting here' and the girls will come. You almost have to take them by the hand and bring them along."

In this situation, the practical problem of dealing with the issue of the involvement of Asian girls in clubs was solved in a practical way initially but subsequently led to a modification of the bland policy objectives of youth provision as set out earlier.

There was a clear recognition in this example that the problem of Asian girls extends beyond the issue of the interests which they share with other girls into the whole problem of dealing with a cultural sub-group of adolescents who are different in their general orientation from the general run of adolescents involved in youth service provision.

What this suggests is that 'decision-makers' viewed the objectives of their policy in their departments in a dispassionate way and irrespective of the cultural nature of the groups in their areas and regarded the issue of appealing to special needs as a practical matter partly because of their sensitivity to the problem of providing separate facilities for separate groups who cannot make use of existing facilities. Only in a few cases were issues such as this permitted to influence and determine the overall policy objectives of departments. One of the councillors in this situation reflected on the difficulty of persuading his colleagues to think about this matter at the highest level of policy by invoking the example of other special groups when he said:

> "I fail to see why they shouldn't have separate facilities. I don't think my colleagues have entirely shared my view on this in the past but as I see it, you can have Scottish country dancing groups, Welsh Presbyterian chapels entirely Welsh-speaking as there are in my ward. Why on earth shouldn't we have separate provision for those young people who feel happier preserving their culture."

Understandably this was very much a minority view.

In point of fact, however, all respondents declared that they have been able to cater for the needs of voluntary groups in their areas. Where such voluntary groups have consisted of uni-racial groups, the youth facilities which they have provided have invariably been used by members of their ethnic group. Thus where uni-racial clubs have emerged, it has been less because of the policy objectives of local authorities and more because of the difficulty of ensuring that voluntary groups maintain a balance between the ethnic groups in the area. Understandably, therefore, few 'decision-makers' were particularly perturbed about the existence of uni-racial youth clubs in their areas though they stressed that they would be unwilling to assist a uni-racial group which deliberately excluded other people and that their ability to assist all voluntary groups is seriously limited by shortage of funds since youth and community work "is one of those things that come at the end of the line when there is any money about."

Thus the flexibility which local authorities allowed themselves in implementing their objectives permitted them to respond to the demands of various interest groups as well as ethnic minority groups in their areas, even though they were in general unwilling to be seen to be providing separate facilities for separate groups as a matter of policy. This sensitivity constitutes an important constraint on youth and community work which must be seen alongside the financial constraints.

Other constraints which emerged during the course of the interviews were:

(a)   the sheer magnitude of demands by large numbers of groups in the inner city which makes it unlikely that sufficient resources of funds and manpower could ever be available to meet such demands even if there were no financial constraints on local authorities, since needs in other areas such as housing and social services invariably command greater priority in most local authorities;

(b)   sociological restraints which create a dilemma as to the content of the activities which should be provided by local and voluntary organisations for modern-day adolescents; as one respondent put it:
"there is a feeling that normal youth provision is no longer related to the way young people live today. Commercial pressures to make them grow up quickly have suggested discos and pubs. What they want is often something which we feel we ought not responsibly to provide; I mean, like a pub or like a rather hot-stuff disco."
As a result, he declared that there is a problem of knowing what exactly to provide as well as where to begin with today's 16 to 20 year olds in general and, indeed, with ethnic minority adolescents who fall into these age limits in particular;

(c)   the inherent confusion in youth and community work between two philosophical strands with very different implications: that is, the participatory principle that young people should be encouraged to involve themselves in the responsibilities of being an adult member of society by taking an active part in the activities of groups of like-minded persons on the one hand and the integration principle — social and racial — on the other hand.

"There are two different philosophical strands involved in youth which have never been clearly separated. One is the participatory principle that young people should be able to do whatever they wish to do because it keeps them out of danger and keeps them away from throwing stones and other kinds of delinquent acts. And there is the second, quite separate, strand which relates to integrating people in the community in which they live either in a multi-racial sense or in a social one. The implications of these two strands are very different."

He went on to stress that the recommendations of the Hunt Report concerning the involvement of ethnic minority adolescents were focused on the second philosphical strand, thus creating a strait-jacket or, as he called it, "this pre-occupation with integration";

(d) the sheer magnitude of the problem of providing adequate staff who can relate to young people as well as to their cultural background. One respondent pointed out that they have been unable to fill vacancies for youth workers — club-based and detached — for the previous eighteen months. Others stressed that not many ethnic minority adolescents are going into youth work training and that even when they do, many of them express a preference for working with groups whose ethnic background they share.

Special Needs of Ethnic Minority Adolescents
While being unwilling to permit the presence of different ethnic groups to determine their overall policy, some of our respondents recognised that ethnic minority adolescents have special needs which are related to their newness to the society, their religious and cultural background and their language deficiency as well as dietary restrictions (in the case of Asians) — all of them factors which militate against their use of existing provision. These needs, they felt, require to be provided for in the short term since in the long term they would either disappear altogether or become attenuated as immigrants become fully absorbed into the gamut of British social life. Indeed, Polish and Ukranian groups were given as examples of immigrant groups whose needs are now attenuated and confined to the area of culture. The problem of appealing to the needs of ethnic minority groups was therefore seen as a temporary one subject to the above-mentioned constraints. But how can these needs be met in the short term?

In order to explore this issue further, we asked them. "Do you think there is a gap between the existing youth service provision and the different needs of different groups of young people?" Most respondents were convinced that there is a gap including those who had discounted the notion of 'special needs' for ethnic minorities. They felt that the education system is coping adequately with these special needs for those between the ages of 14 and 16 and that the problems arise only when adolescents — both ethnic minorities and indigenous — leave school at sixteen. The gap is therefore confined to the older adolescents. It was for this reason that they felt that futher progress can be made by relating youth provision to the education system so as to ensure continuity between friendships at school and friendships in the 'out of school context'. To what extent were special needs articulated by the other respondents in the survey (i.e. club-based workers, detached youth workers and the young people themselves)?

Special Needs — Youth Workers
All the professional youth-workers agreed that there were special problems pertaining to each sub-group of ethnic minorities which require more attention than they have received in the past. We can best illustrate some of these problems by quoting from the interview transcipts:

(1)   **West Indians**
    "...left to face a problem alone ... because 50% of West Indian families are one-parent families"

    "Discrimination on account of colour — black is worse than brown"

    "First generation West Indians are strong disciplinarians and have a strong moral code which cause extreme conflict with present day youngsters whose life now is more liberal"

    "Problems with behaviour towards white people and their acceptance of whites, especially of females. Cultural and parental background causes difficulties."

    "I get the feeling it's not West Indian to be clever at the moment."

(2)   **Asians from India/Pakistan**
    "Asians especially girls, living in a free, even permissive society have conflict against their own family and cultural backgrounds"

    "They tend to be less aware of the provisions available and how to 'exploit' them, they are rather suspicious of any form of officials"

    "Because of their extreme sense of morality, this has implications for young Asian boys who may want to go with other youths to youth clubs or pubs — due to religious and family background"

    "To the parents, a 'club' is a place to drink and smoke so we will have to change the name; the authority won't recognise this. The girls need a separate evening to encourage them to come out."

"Asians will not mix on the whole with other groups. There are language difficulties and difficulties of different origin within their own group"

(3) **Asians from East Africa**
"I don't think there is much difference apart from Asians from East Africa who think they are a bit above the rest"

"Settle in better because they have been used to more of our type of life in Kenya"

"They have experienced a loss in status which they find hard to live with"

(4) **Cypriots**
"Extremely tight group and if threatened, they react violently"

"They're resented by blacks and whites alike. Their business acumen being a sore point ... the females are too cloistered and unable to mix with blokes. The men and boys are very aggressive and cause more discipline problems. They're very arrogant and offensive"

"They're not disadvantaged in the same sense ... they don't have problems of employment"

"There is no colour problem, however, there are problems — language and culture wise"

Unlike most of the 'decision-makers', only in one isolated case was a respondent unwilling to discuss the separate groups and their problems. He said:
"I find it difficult to draw lines here — I never think of any of our members as being of different origins or ethnic origins. I'm not seeing them as coloured, or immigrants but simply as human beings."

In sum, almost all the professional practitioners were aware of the special problems which pertain to various people of ethnic minority adolescents in their areas and saw their role as providing some support:
"Helping individuals with personal and home problems"

"Discussions and getting them to talk about themselves, and theories on their own identities. We can act as liaison officer with the careers office as far as employment and with the CRC as far as housing is concerned"

"Counsellor, friend, adviser, educator"

112

Those who are detached youth workers explained the advantages of their role by saying:

"As a detached worker you don't have to spend so much time in administration. There is more face to face contact and you can respond very flexibly to changing needs. More independent of the authority."

"In a club you work with a group. Detached, you work with a certain kid on an individual basis"

"It's difficult for a club leader to go into the background of the children the way I do — I can meet parents too"

"I go to meet these boys at their base and this makes a lot of difference. This makes him feel I have an interest in him"

Our professional practitioners were drawn from both ethnic minorities and from indigenous youth workers. It may therefore be supposed, and often is, that their ethnic background plays a part in (a) the groups of adolescents they work with (b) their ability to work with different ethnic groups. We explored these issues in the interviews and found that there was no significant tendency for youth workers from ethnic minority backgrounds to work with groups drawn from their own ethnic background. Indeed, only 2 white youth workers worked with exclusively white adolescents and 6 black and Asian workers worked with exclusively black or Asian adolescents; the rest worked with mixed groups. In the case of the few who worked with exclusively uni-racial groups, the reasons given were that youth leaders had been provided by the authority for other ethnic groups or that the problems of ethnic minority adolescents were greater. They all agreed that the only context in which the ethnic background of a youth worker may be significant is in connection with making contacts with adolescents:

"Initial contact and breakthrough is important. After that one has to be professional all the way and any white or black professional could handle this"

If the initial contact and breakthrough is important, it is because most youth workers have to face considerable suspicion from adolescents. One ethnic minority practitioner respondent reflected this by saying:

"If a white person walks in and says 'I'm a doctor', OK. If I walk in and say 'I'm a doctor', then I'm on trial until I can prove myself"

Another (white) respondent reflected the same thing by saying:

"Being a white woman, makes a difference but I have to bear with it and be patient. Prove yourself to be different from their initial conception of you."

It may further be supposed from this, that their training would have prepared them for situations such as this one. In order to find out, we asked them whether they feel that their training had been useful to them in their work. Only 33% of our respondents claimed that it had. Those who felt it had been inadequate explained that:

"There was too much emphasis on the theoretical side"

"...did not cover working with immigrant groups"

"No mention of ethnic minorities or detached youth work"

"Because I don't think there can ever be an adequate training. It's a question of experience and personality"

"Training is unrelated to the present needs of areas like..."

"Unsatisfactory — the qualification bar has stopped certain deserving people from obtaining qualifications"

"Abysmal, a real reluctance to depart from traditional historical understanding of youth worker's role."

"Good for main stream youth workers but for specialist areas such as detached youth workers, specialist courses are essential"

Experience of Youth Clubs — Youth's Response

In order to establish the range of experience as well as on-going patterns of usage of youth clubs by our adolescent respondents (ethnic and whites), we explored their attachment to youth clubs as well as the reasons for either attending them or not attending them.

Only about a third of our respondents had ever been to a youth club in the past but, and significantly, only 11% still attend. This figure is much lower than the figure of 26% reported by Margaret Bone and the bulk of that difference is accounted for by ethnic minority adolescents not attending. Among all ethnic minority adolescents, Asians from Pakistan, East Africa and Hindus are less likely ever to have been involved in a youth club compared to Cypriots or West Indians. The majority of those who attend or had been attached to youth clubs had been involved with sports clubs organised by their school or education authority, their churches or some religious body.

The reasons for attending youth clubs are however less interesting than the reasons which were advanced by those who do not attend youth clubs. A third of those who do not (and never did) attend a youth club said that it was because there is none in the areas in which they live and a further quarter said that they are not interested in going to a youth club, have never attended one and a fifth have no time to attend one. In other words, the majority of those who do not attend account for that in terms of reasons which are not connected with youth clubs in general. This was brought into even sharper relief when they were asked whether they had ever met youth workers other than in a club situation; only one in ten had ever done so thus re-inforcing the need for more detached youth workers which a few of the 'decision-makers' stressed. Granted that these adolescents could ever be involved in youth clubs, what kind of clubs would like?

The majority of respondents (whites and ethnic) wanted a club "where people are friendly and sociable" and which is a sports club. There was no difference between the sexes in this response. However, within that pattern, Cypriots were most likely to want sports clubs and white British and West Indians least likely. Only 5% wanted a club for their own ethnic group exclusively or one with more of their own ethnic group in it. When discussion of their ideal club was broadened out into an exploration of their perception of such facilities as exist in their areas, one in three said that there were no facilities at all and a further one in five said that the facilities were inadequate. Only 3% said that the facilities in their areas were good.

Within this pattern of response, Asians from Pakistan and East Africa were least likely to *complain* about the facilities or lack of them compared to other ethnic groups. But among all Asians, Sikhs were more critical than the others. When asked what facilities they would like to see in their areas, three out of ten respondents desired sports clubs — a response which did not vary with areas or language groups. Dances and discos were the second most popular response though Asians were less likely to mention them than the others.

Summary

Our discussion in this chapter has highlighted a number of issues. Firstly, a low priority is given to youth and community work by local authorities compared to their other responsibilities.

Secondly, the flexibility of the approach which is adopted should, in theory, enable local authorities to cope with youth provision for ethnic minority group members who have special needs which prevent them from involving themselves in existing youth provision; in reality, however, few 'decision-makers' have apparently either worked out or dealt with the logical implications of their flexible approach as it affects ethnic minority groups partly because of the financial constraints which impinge on their work and partly because of their sensitivity to the issue as to whether special facilies should be provided for special groups where such groups are ethnic rather than interest groups.

Thirdly, all our respondents ('decision-makers') were aware of the recommendations of the Hunt Report as it affects ethnic minority groups but a number of them suggested that the Hunt Report may have added to the confusion which has always existed in youth work insofar as it stressed the participatory principle as well as the multi-racial integration principle, without exploring the implications of these two very different philosophical strands; one respondent added that it also created the false dichotomy between uni-racial clubs and multi-racial clubs in a situation in which both types of provision are required and also subscribed to the idea that the provision of uni-racial clubs for those groups who require it is somehow peripheral and anti-thetical to the provision of multi-racial clubs:

"I think the issue is whether to provide totally integrated facilities and not encourage any separate facilities or the other way round. My view is there's a need for both. There is a need for facilities which are clearly in no way segregated and a need for facilities which are."

Another respondent reflected the difficulty which this dichotomy can create when he talked about the difficulty of ensuring an adequate balance in the racial composition of youth clubs over a period of time and said:

"Since membership of a youth organisation is a voluntary one, it is very difficult to say that a club or an organisation should have, say, 10% West Indians or 10% Asians and so on. It is very difficult to preserve a a balance however desirable this might be"

This issue of the ethnic or racial balance of a club arises from the emphasis in the Hunt Report on the integration principle. To be sure, only 5% of the adolescents (ethnic minority and whites) we interviewed desired a club which is exclusively confined to their own ethnic group; in the main, their orientations were towards multi-racialism, but many of our 'decision-makers' respondents felt that the emphasis on multi-racialism in the Hunt Report is over-stated and ignores the practical fact that uni-racial clubs are more suitable to some adolescents than multi-racial clubs. The further fact that the adolescents we interviewed uniformly stressed that they liked the youth leaders they have been involved with, irrespective of the ethnic background of these leaders, suggests that there are sizeable numbers of ethnic minority adolescents who are themselves interested in multi-racial clubs. It is the over-emphasis in the Hunt Report on multi-racialism which 'decision-makers' found an unnecessary constraint.

Fourthly, a small proportion of all the adolescents we interviewed (11%) were attending youth clubs though a larger number had been involved in the past. Among those from ethnic minority groups, larger numbers and significantly more Asians have never ever been involved in youth provision nor are presently involved in youth clubs in spite of the over-representation of all ethnic minority adolescents among all adolescents in the 14 to 20 age group which we stressed earlier (i.e. three ethnic minority adolescents for every one

116

white British adolescent fell within this age group in 1971).

Finally, the majority of our professional respondents (i.e. youth workers) recognised that ethnic minority adolescents had special problems and special needs which require support — one-parent families, language deficiency, dietary restrictions, problems of identity and suspicion of authority figures etc. However, whereas only one youth worker was unwilling to consider his charges from the point of view of their special needs, the majority of 'decision-makers' were sensitive about recognising special needs among ethnic minority adolescents or recognising that such special problems as apply to ethnic minorities result in either a need for special provision or for modifications of the policy objectives of their departments.

Chapter Six: Social Services and Ethnic Minority Communities

The issue as to whether to make separate provision for ethnic minorities as against the indigenous community which we have highlighted in the previous chapter is brought into even sharper relief in the area of the social services where the traditional orientation of social work and social workers, social service departments and the very central notion of providing help to deprived and disadvantaged groups has had to contend with the presence of ethnic minority groups whose cultural backgrounds and religious prescriptions are very different from those of the indigenous communities. Even the notion of family support in welfare matters has a different implication for ethnic minority groups as we show later (e.g. Asian groups) from that which operates among the indigenous communities. The combination of these issues (those deriving from the orientation of social work and social services departments and those deriving from the background of ethnic minority groups) has raised a whole series of questions as to whether ethnic minority groups are using the social services to the same extent as their indigenous counterparts, whether the social services are geared to providing for their needs, whether sufficient staff with sufficient skill and training for dealing with the problems of both ethnic minority and indigenous communities is available and, indeed, whether social work training has been sufficiently adapted to the presence of ethnic minority groups. These questions have been of considerable concern to policy-makers, professional practitioners and, indeed, to all those who have been concerned with the issue of equal rights and equal access to welfare facilities.

In this chapter, we shall turn our attention to these questions and illustrate the issues which they raise by drawing on the findings of our surveys of policy 'decision-makers', professional practitioners (social workers) and laymen in our eight project areas. In doing so, we shall be able to demonstrate (a) the extent to which the social services have responded, or failed to respond, to the presence of ethnic minority groups in urban areas, (b) the extent to which these groups are disadvantaged in gaining access to those services which are relevant to their needs and (c) the extent to which their needs are the same as or are different from those of the indigenous population.

The Professional Context and Orientation of the Social Services
It is as well to begin by outlining the professional context and orientation of

the social services in Britain since these constitute an important constraining factor in the extent to which they can be adapted to meet the needs of ethnic minorities.

The context and orientation of the social services are determined by two important considerations. Firstly, and in contrast to educational and health services, the social services are not provided as a universal service for the whole population irrespective of need. On the contrary, they are offered only to that sector of the population — a minority to be sure — who have 'demonstrated' their need for support and assistance by the conditions in which they live and by the problems which they experience. In this respect, the majority of the population are assumed to be able to manage their home, social affairs and relationships on their own without the assistance of the social services. Some of the people identified as clients of the social services are more or less in constant need of assistance — the handicapped, the elderly, certain multi-problem families — while others are normally self-reliant but need assistance only during an emergency or crisis, such as death or illness.

A second factor of relevance is that social service departments do not usually identify their clients in terms of their racial or religious backgrounds; to do so would run counter to the idea of a personal service which assesses and meets individual needs. People may be grouped by social workers because they share a common disadvantage: for example, single-parent families, the disabled — but the grouping follows the identification of need rather than precedes it. Accordingly, social workers tend to think of individual members of ethnic minority groups as belonging to client categories. This point was stressed by our respondents during the 'decision-makers' interviews:

"We have coloured old people in homes for the aged but no homes specifically for coloured old people"

"We make provision for problems that arise among groups. If these problems arise within a particular ethnic group, then within the case context, we shall look at them. I don't think we ever really consider problems as being particular to particular ethnic groups. If this does occur, then we will try to make adequate provision but we don't say 'Well, we have a black problem; we must now make provision for that problem'."

"We do not make special exception for immigrants or treat them as a special group. We are concerned to improve our services and make them more relevant to the socially deprived as a whole and that includes immigrants."

Given this conceptual background to social work, a measure of the disadvantage of ethnic minority groups in relation to social services is the extent to which they use available provisions and the extent to which they predominate in client categories. Non-use, in this context, may indicate a tendency towards self-reliance among those who are disadvantaged. On the other hand, it may indicate conditions less satisfactory: a shortage of social work services in areas of greatest need, a lack of flexibility in recognising and responding to new needs, a failure to provide services in an appealing manner, a shortage of adequately skilled staff, etc.

Use Made of Social Services by Ethnic Minority Groups

There is no general, systematic data on the use of the social services, and particularly, no data which covers the ethnic or racial origins of clients. Each social service department will keep case files, and if its social workers consider it relevant to the case, such case records may include a reference to the country of origin of the client. These case records, which are confidential, are not used to compile statistics on the use made of the social services by various groups but are kept for practical case work only.

Nevertheless, some information is available from small, local studies about the use made of the social services by members of ethnic minority groups. For example, the London Borough of Wandsworth produced figures for the period between 1 November 1973 and 31st January 1974 which showed that 48% of all children received into care were of West Indian origin.[1] These figures also showed that the reasons for reception into care varied between West Indian and British children, and that West Indian children tended to be younger.

A survey of children in residential homes undertaken by Association of British Adoption Agencies noted that one in four children in residential homes are black or of mixed race. Figures taken from the 1971 Census of persons enumerated in children's homes in Greater London showed two boroughs where there were more children of New Commonwealth origin living in residential homes than indigenous children, and fourteen boroughs where more than one in four children in these homes were of New Commonwealth parentage.

A survey undertaken by Peter Boss and Jane Homeshaw of the Leicester University School of Social Work on "Coloured Families and Social Services Departments" in Leicester found that proportionately fewer 'coloured' people approached social services departments than did the rest of the population. This was particularly true of Indians, less than 0.1% of whom visited the department. West Indians on the other hand, were twice as likely to visit the department as were the population as a whole (1.03% West Indians visited, as compared with 0.53% of the total population).[2] It also showed that ethnic minority clients usually approach social services departments about child reception into care, and less often about child offences, school refusal, accommodation and financial difficulties, than other clients. It also found that case-work with ethnic minority clients did not take up more time than case-work with other clients, and that 'coloured' clients were less likely to return to social workers for help in the future than were white clients. This is also confirmed by the experience of community relations fieldworkers who report that ethnic minority clients rarely approach social services departments except for assistance with children (reception into care, fostering, day care, etc).

Related to this is the range of difficulties of one-parent families, who tend to make a greater use of social services departments than people in other categories of need. In other areas of social work, such as work with the disabled or the elderly, there tend to be few ethnic minority clients.

Our surveys among policy 'decision-makers' and professional social workers revealed a considerable awareness of the fact that ethnic minority groups in their areas utilise the social services less than their representation in the population in their areas would lead one to expect and featured in some client categories more than they do in others. The reasons for this are numerous and have to do with their cultural backgrounds and their emphasis on self-support within their communities, reasons which we shall expand on later in this chapter.

However, there was one implication of their relatively lower level of use, compared to their indigenous counterparts, which was stressed by policy 'decision-makers'. Since the social services are administered in terms of personal need, social service departments are forced to allocate higher priority to those clients and needs which are *pressed* upon them. In this way, the effective demand for social services in an area tends to ensure that social workers in those areas attribute higher priority towards meeting those needs which are vociferously articulated. In this way, other needs which exist in the community and which may be more directly related to the cultural, religious and racial background of groups either tend to be ignored or are given lower priority. One respondent illustrated this by saying:

> "Our social workers have been overwhelmed by the problems which were brought into our area by the overspill population from ... (place mentioned). These people, their problems and their families have been more of a worry and concern to us than are those immigrants who live in this district"

He went on to stress the danger that can arise from the pull of effective demand by saying:

> "Of course there is the danger that immigrants' needs may be overlooked because they do not make as much fuss as the others".

In other words, the pull of effective demand by the more vociferous groups can influence the priorities of social workers and social services departments. This has undoubtedly constrained the ability of social services departments to react to those needs which exist but have not been articulated by ethnic minority groups on the one hand and has contributed to the lower level of use of the social services by ethnic minority groups on the other.

Another respondent reflected on the lower level of use of the social services by ethnic minority groups and touched on the need for a new orientation at the level of policy-making to deal with this particular matter, when he said:

"I very much doubt whether any elderly Asian immigrants go to the luncheon clubs in this area. It may well be that we'll have to start thinking of setting up separate services for immigrants as against our earlier hostility towards this idea for it is very clear that elderly Asians in this area have nowhere to go during the daytime".

He went on to stress that this was very much a private view and one which was highly unpopular in his council and among his colleagues. In other words, some of the earlier assumptions involved in the provision of services by social services departments are beginning to be questioned in the face of the emergence of needs pertaining to ethnic minorities. Further, it is becoming evident in many areas that various assumptions which were made about the ability of ethnic minority groups to contain their problems within the family — the problem of battered wives among Asians or the ability of Asians to absorb their elderly relatives — are being proved to be false as the tight Asian family structure responds to social life in Britain by disintegrating somewhat. Even the problem of one-parent families which was, at one time assumed to be unknown among Asians, is beginning to emerge. Similarly the emergence of elderly Asians in some old people's homes is beginning to call for a re-appraisal of the presentation of services for ethnic minority clients (e.g. "curry on wheels") and Kosher meals for elderly Jews.

However, the view that special consideration should be given to those needs which affect ethnic minorities directly or affect them more than indigenous clients was an unpopular one during our 'decision-makers' interviews. Many of our respondents were worried that such consideration would either destroy or seriously attenuate the contextual basis and orientation of social service departments and social workers. Others were worried about being seen to 'discriminate' in favour of some groups as against others. Yet others were worried that such special consideration may be the beginning of the slippery slope towards the creation of segregated institutions for different ethnic groups. As a result, few policy-makers reported that this issue had been discussed in their councils or recognised that there is a continuum between providing services for everybody without regard to apparently extraneous matters such as race on the one hand and setting up racially segregated 'apartheid' institutions on the other hand.

One respondent who had clearly worked out the implications of this question suggested that such thinking by local authorities may reveal an area of ignorance which they may be unable to handle when he said:

"I personally do not think that this Borough has either the expertise or the resources to fully work through some of the needs and their implications among ethnic minority groups. ... I'm not quite sure that if we even had all the money we require, we would know where to begin, where to start and what's required. So it's not quite right to say that we are limited by resource considerations alone. I'm just wondering, where do we start, what are the needs and how do you define them? I think we know what the needs are in housing, and education. In these areas you can measure needs; it's like job evaluation; you can actually measure them but the social services, it's a much more difficult and complex matter"

He went on to suggest that outside assistance would be required with this problem in the long term but added that in the short term:

"My own personal feeling is that if we had the resources, we would probably get a special team of social workers/community workers who are especially knowledgeable about ... (minority group mentioned) who will operate in the community in a detached role and refer immigrants with special needs to the relevant agency, sort out and define those needs which are different from those we have dealt with in the past, sort out the unregistered child-minders and refer them to the local authority to be trained and supported..."

The tenor of this suggestion clearly implies that the unpopularity of the notion of giving special thought or consideration to those needs which are either specific to ethnic minorities or impinge on them more than indigenous people is not only due to the political caution and professional commitment of 'decision-makers' or, indeed, to their sensitivity about being seen to 'discriminate'; it also implies that there is a fear of opening a Pandora's box of problems as well and possibly raising expectations and/or stimulating a demand for services which cannot be supported within existing resources. The result is that most 'decision-makers' declared that their authorities have always been willing to consider making such adaptations to existing services as would meet the needs of specific ethnic or religious groups of people as an administrative or practical matter (e.g. providing Kosher meals in Old People's Homes for those which contain elderly Jews) but not as a matter of policy.

By contrast, we interviewed professional social workers in the eight project areas and found that only 9% were unwilling to consider the issue of special needs of ethnic minority groups or did not recognise that there were respects in which the typical approach adopted by the profession requires to be changed, modified or adapted. Similarly, only a minority felt that the content of the training which they had received enabled them to operate with both ethnic minority and indigenous clients.

Some Special Needs of Ethnic Minorities

It will be recalled that while the issue of special needs was considered by policy 'decision-makers' to raise merely administrative and practical issues rather than policy ones, the professional social workers we interviewed saw them as requiring greater emphasis on the level of policy making. Only 10% of those we interviewed in our practitioner survey felt that ethnic minority groups were evenly distributed across all categories of need. The rest felt that they featured more in some categories of need than in others. The areas mentioned were: the need for improved diet among Hindu Asians in particular, language problems which affect communication and support by social workers, the problem of conflict between parents and children among ethnic minorities, the problem of the isolation of Asian women (especially Muslim women), the need for considerable advice and referral to other agencies, the need to handle the tension generated by arranged marriages among Asians, the fragmentation of the family structure of ethnic minorities (including Asians), one-parent families and the need for more varied child care services. Those need areas to which particular emphasis were given in the interviews were: (a) the elderly (b) one-parent families and family support work (c) children in care and (d) the need for day care facilities. We shall now examine the wider parameters of these need areas in turn and the pattern of social service support they point to.

(a) The Elderly

As has already been mentioned, there are fewer elderly people among ethnic minorities. Nevertheless, 59,010 elderly people were born in a New Commonwealth country and of these 26,400 had parents who were born in the New Commonwealth. Table 16 shows the country of birth of these people. The distribution of this group of New Commonwealth over-60-year-olds follows that of the ethnic minority communities to which they belong; over 60% live in the South East and 35% in Greater London.

TABLE 16: Elderly People from Ethnic Minorities

		Men	Women
New Commonwealth	26,400	14,000	12,400
India	11,600	6,700	4,900
Pakistan	1,400	1,200	200
West Indies	6,600	3,300	3,300
Cyprus	3,000	1,600	1,400
Africa	900	500	400

Many of the needs of these people are similar to those of other old people living in the inner-city: low incomes, poor housing, social isolation, problems of adjustment to old age, poor health and impaired mobility.

However, ethnic minority old people have special needs over and above their shared difficulties as was demonstrated in Age Concern's 'Elderly Ethnic Minorities'.[3] These are firstly, their insecurity in a new environment, their remoteness from friends and relations, their different cultural background and difficulties in establishing new neighbourhood and community networks to replace those broken through migration. Secondly, there are needs arising from racial discrimination and prejudice, which lead to an increased sense of isolation and rejection which, in turn, make it less likely that black elderly people will feel free to make use of facilities provided by local authorities. Thirdly, there are difficulties arising from the contrast between the expectation of care that ethnic minority old people would have received within their families in their home country and the realities of care in Britain. In the home context, although there are obvious differences between India, Pakistan, Bangladesh, Cyprus and the West Indies, there is a general emphasis on care within the family, and an old person can not only expect care, but also commands respect and authority within the extended family household and in the community at large.

With the changes in family patterns occurring through adjustment to conditions in Britain — for example, overcrowding in housing which leads to smaller family units, or an increasing incidence of working wives — the elderly among ethnic minorities find themselves increasingly left alone and without a status or role in the family and in the society. Considerable unhappiness and distress is caused by elderly immigrants' unrealised expectations of family-centred care and their experience of loneliness and neglect in a society which places emphasis on corporate care for old people.

(b) One-Parent Families

The incidence of one-parent families differs in different ethnic minority communities. The available evidence indicates that there are proportionately more one-parent families in the West Indian community. In the West Indies, there is a variety of socially-approved patterns of conjugal relationships and parenthood, and illegitimacy rates (as usually defined in this country) are high. Accordingly, women frequently take responsibility for financially supporting their families. In the social context of the West Indies, such children in fatherless families are not considered disadvantaged.

With migration to Britain, relatively higher proportions of West Indians are able to gain sufficient command over resources to take on the commitment of marriage, and, compared with the West Indies, very small proportions remain unmarried while living in England. Taking examples from local studies, Hood et al. found in Paddington that 65% of West Indian mothers were married and 14% were in stable cohabitation.[4] Moody and Stroud[5] found in their sample of 100 mothers from the West Indies that 85 were married; Pollak[6] in Brixton found that 73% of West Indian mothers were married and 7% were in stable cohabitation; only 1% were living alone.

Nevertheless, and despite a high rate of marriage among West Indians in Britain, it is still more common for West Indian children to be in one-parent families than for indigenous children. A literacy survey of 35,000 children in ILEA schools in 1968 showed that 13% of West Indian children were in one-parent families compared with 8% British children. A survey of one-parent families in Haringey showed that 20% of unmarried mothers were West Indian, while West Indians formed only 10% of two-parent families. This survey also showed that the reason for this over-representation of West Indian one-parent families was not a higher rate of marital breakdown in West Indian families, but was due to the existence of a large number of unmarried, never-married, West Indian mothers.[7]

The comparatively high percentage of one-parent West Indian families does not exhaust the implications for social services of the carry-over of West Indian family patterns to Britain with migration. There are two other important consequences: firstly, many West Indian single mothers emigrated to England, and left their children with relatives. The children were the financial responsibility of the mother, who supported them through remitted savings. These mothers have invariably married or formed stable relationships in England and have had more children from these unions. Despite their marriage and financial dependence on their husbands, it is not unusual for West Indian mothers to retain responsibility for financially supporting their children in the West Indies. In this way, married West Indian women often share some of the difficulties and problems of one-parent families, in their need for an independent income. Secondly, the West Indian male may also have had children prior to his marriage in this country and may be supporting them; accordingly, he cannot use all his disposable income to support his wife and family here.

These factors have a great effect on the finances of West Indian families: for example, Hood et al. found that over 50% of West Indian families in their sample in Paddington were supporting children living outside the home. 10 of the 23 children in Stewart Prince's study had mother who had responsibilities for children left in the West Indies.[8] 47 of the 100 West Indian mothers in Moody and Stroud's survey had children who were not living at home. Pollack also found that West Indian men gave less money to their wives for housekeeping than English men with similar incomes: over 60% of West Indian men gave their wives £8.50, whereas 60% of English men gave £12.5—£20 per week at the time when she did her survey. These additional financial commitments for the support of children outside the home render West Indian families vulnerable to financial stringency and its attendant crisis.

One-parent families are less common among Asians than among West Indians, and among the indigenous population. Estimates from the 1971 Census suggest that there may be about 5,000 households (about 1% of the total Asian population) where the parent is divorced, separated or widowed. The ILEA survey quoted earlier suggests that 6.3% of Indian children and 7.2% Pakistani children in London have one-parent families. The East African Asian community are likely to have rather more widows and widowers, since as refugees, they had no choice but to come to this country whereas in normal circumstances they may not have chosen to migrate.

There are growing numbers of reports that a few Asian teenagers, often largely brought up in this country and often in conflict with their parents and community, become pregnant. In such an event, their major concern is usually to cover up and disguise the deeply felt shame accruing to the family and community. Either an abortion or an adoption will be arranged. The majority of one-parent Asian families will therefore consist of widows, separated or divorced parents. However, although there may be proportionately fewer one-parent families, there is no pattern of self-reliant, mother-headed families in the Asian community as there is in the West Indian community. Consequently, the needs of the one-parent Asian family may be great. Special difficulties may be experienced by Asian women who are without the assistance of relatives, extended family or community, who face particular difficulties in both providing for their family and in child-rearing. Reared to see themselves as dependants (of their fathers or their husbands), it may be difficult for such women to take on a bread-winning, head of family role.

(c) Child Care
In a number of local authorities, children born to parents of New Commonwealth origin form a high proportion of the child population. For example, in 1972, over a third of the children born in Haringey, Brent and Hackney were of New Commonwealth origin, as were over 20% of births in Islington, Wandsworth, Lambeth, Hammersmith, Newham and Birmingham. It can be expected therefore, that a high proportion of ethnic minority children in these areas will be in need of care and fostering facilities.

Research has identified several characteristics of natural parents which pre-dispose them to seek child-care facilities for their children, and these factors affect all socially and economically disadvantaged groups in the population regardless of race or colour. The natural parents of children in care have been found to be disproportionately drawn from the lower social classes with low incomes. They have more often been lone parents, under 30 years old when their children were 'received' into care, have been subject to frequent moves of housing, were living in inferior housing conditions (especially with regard to overcrowding) and without the support of kin. In each of these categories, ethnic minorities are over-represented due to the special difficulties they face through migration and through racial discrimination.

Other factors which lead to a need for assistance with child care among ethnic minority communities are varied: the West Indian family's obligations to support children outside the home (referred to earlier) represents a high-risk factor for other children in the family e.g. financial strains, worry and psychological stress over separation, the mothers' need for an independent income leading her to take up outside employment and thus having to pay high fees for the day care of her pre-school children, the stresses in the family when the 'outside' children eventually join the family; all these strains can undermine the ability of the parents (especially the mothers) to cope.

West Africans in Britain face a dilemma deriving from two very strong but contradictory motivations. The majority of West Africans in this country are students. At the same time, there is a strong motivation to have a family; as a result, there is a high degree of need for child care facilities for the children of West African students where either both spouses are studying full-time, or where one is working full-time to support the other in his studies.[9]

In the Asian community, there are two main reasons why families need assistance with child care. One is when the mother suffers illness; and the other is when the parents are absent from the home when paying visits to Asia to fulfil family obligations (e.g. nursing sick parents, or sorting out affairs after the death of their relatives). As was shown earlier, the majority of Asians in Britain are separated from their parents who remain in Asia. There are also growing indications that changes within the Asian family are leading to family breakdown with the result that increasing proportions of Asian children are being received into care. Mixed race children are predisposed to be in need of care due to a combination of poverty and parental rejection.

(d) Day Care

The need for services to look after children during the day time are closely related to the pressures on families described above: ill-health in the family, inadequate housing, strain resulting in mothers being unable to cope, one-parent families, all present needs for children to have access to a day nursery environment as part of assisting the family to resolve its difficulties. Ethnic minorities are over-represented in families which are disadvantaged in these ways.

A need for day care also arises when families with low incomes have to keep their families together, by the mother going out to work to supplement the family's income. The 1971 Census recorded growing numbers of mothers going out to work, and over 90% of the mothers of pre-school children at work were doing so in order to supplement their families' incomes. Ethnic minority families are over-represented among low-income families; accordingly, the mothers of young children in such families are more likely to be at work and to work for longer hours, than are other mothers. This was illustrated by the Runnymede Trust Census Project (Lomas & Monck op. cit.) which found that 85% of 'coloured' mothers of children under five are at work in Leicester, 77% in Manchester, 44% in Bradford and 41% in Wolverhampton — this compares with a national average of 50% for all mothers of children under five.[10] Whereas the majority of white mothers worked under 30 hours, in Bradford, Leicester and Manchester, over 75% of 'coloured' mothers worked over 30 hours a week.

The indications then, are that ethnic minority families are much more in need of day care assistance than are other families in the population as a whole.

Community and Family Support
Immigrants to Britain from New Commonwealth countries are 'geared' to be self-reliant in meeting their own needs since they come from countries which are not welfare states and which do not have highly developed social services. In their countries of origin, individuals in need of assistance would be able to call on family or community networks, and would reciprocate with assistance to other relatives. However, ethnic minority families in Britain are no more than fragments of extended family units in their countries of origin and physical separation disrupts reciprocal relationships within such families. It is particularly in the loss of relatives who usually provide extensive support in child care — grandmothers, aunts, older female relatives — that ethnic minority families are affected.

Nevertheless, considerable assistance is given within ethnic minority communities in Britain. The extent to which families in need of advice or assistance turn first or by preference to such sources rather than to social services or other agencies was investigated in our survey of laymen (ethnic minorities and indigenous) for this project. We found that only four in ten of our ethnic minority respondents were aware of housing aid and other advice centres as against eight out of ten of our indigenous respondents. Further, we found that whereas 39% of our indigenous sample had been in a position in which they needed advice, the proportions of ethnic minority respondents who claimed to have been in this position varied from 42% of the West Indians, 43% of the Cypriots, 32% of the Pakistanis, 30% of the Indians and 28% of the East African Asians. In such a situation, higher proportions of the Asian groups turned to friends and relatives for such advice as was needed compared to the indigenous group and West Indians.

A further factor of relevance in considering unmet need among ethnic minority communities is the extent to which the community are able to meet their own needs. In the case of the arrival of Ugandan refugees in 1972, a Resettlement Board was set up by the Government. The facilities of this agency were used, to some extent, by about 21,000 Ugandan Asians out of a total of 28,000 arriving; and about 11,000 were eventually resettled by the Uganda Resettlement Board (i.e. they obtained accommodation through the services of the Board). The majority of refugees, however, were settled by the self-help initiatives of the Asian community, particularly the East African Asian community who had previously settled in this country. The refugees settled by self-help include the 7,000 or so who went straight from the airport on arrival to the community, and a further 10,000 who spent some time in resettlement camps, but who made their own arrangements to settle in the community. The settlement of these 17,000 refugees thus provides a useful measure of the self-help capacity of the Asian community. In fact, research conducted by the Community Relations Commission[11] into the resettlement of Uganda Asians revealed that community assistance was more valuable overall than government and local authority services, in helping refugees to feel at home and to settle in this country.

Further, refugees relied heavily on the help of friends and relatives in exploring opportunities, in finding jobs, housing, schools and other amenities. They also found, in their community, the personal friendships and support they needed to rebuild their confidence after the traumas of evacuation. Those refugees who were denied access to this community support (because they were dispersed by the URB) suffered considerable difficulties as a result. On the other hand, where resources were in short supply in the receiving community, the refugees settled by self-help were at a disadvantage to those resettled officially; this was particularly true of housing where the Asian community, though willing to receive refugees into their homes, had insufficient access to housing resources to provide accommodation. The refugees resettled in local authority housing fared better than self-settled refugees in their conditions of housing and accommodation. The resettlement of Ugandan refugees thus illustrates some of the limitations of both community self-help and of officially provided social services in meeting the needs of this ethnic minority group.

Staffing and Training — 'Decision-makers' and Practitioners

In order to round out our exploration of the use of social services by ethnic minorities, we explored the constraints under which policy 'decision-makers' work and social workers' views on the extent to which their training enables them to cope with the requirements and demands of indigenous and ethnic minority clients in urban areas.

Most of our policy 'decision-makers' felt that they had had to devise their policies in their areas under financial constraints, under staffing constraints, under the constraints of not appearing to discriminate in favour of any particular group and, in one isolated case, under the constraint of not fully knowing what the specific needs of ethnic minorities are, how these needs manifest themselves and how they can be handled within the present context and orientation of social work.

With regard to finance, it was recognised that financial resources at any one point in time are likely to be limited and that priorities have to be worked out with this in mind. However, no respondent felt that Urban Aid has been useful in this particular connection for a variety of reasons. Firstly, they felt that the administrative arrangements for submitting and processing Urban Aid applications ignore the priorities of local social services departments; in this regard, one respondent declared that Urban Aid is "the most half-witted system that can ever have been devised".

Secondly, its 'pump-priming' role means that local authorities must be prepared to take over the cost of running Urban Aid Projects when the Home Office's contribution of 75% of costs is withdrawn after the first three to five years (according to the length of time for which its grants was made) or abandon the project because of the difficulty of bearing the costs. Even the 25% contribution of local authorities is usually difficult to find especially as Urban Aid Project applications relate to projects which would normally not fall within the priorities of local authorities. In other words, while Urban Aid is designed to support projects which local authorities may not otherwise feel obliged to carry out, it operates in such a way that they end up bearing the full cost of providing a service which was never initially high on their list of priorities. For this reason, one respondent described it as "one huge con trick". Indeed, the level of dissatisfaction with Urban Aid was so widespread that it is clear that Urban Aid has not been found to be particularly useful by local authorities.

With regards to staffing, all our respondents deplored the general scarcity of well trained staff who can operate with both ethnic minority and indigenous clients in inner city areas. We have already referred to unfilled vacancies for youth workers with expertise in dealing with ethnic minority adolescents in the last chapter. This situation, would appear to be general across various areas and especially in the social services.

In this regard, our respondents recognised that the presence of ethnic minority clients in their areas has implications for the skills which social workers in these areas should have as well as for their training even while rejecting the possibility that their specific needs require specific and separate policy action. For this reason, all our respondents recognised the need to recruit social workers with an understanding of the background and problems of ethnic minority clients; they also recognised that the approach adopted by a social worker with an ethnic minority client cannot be the same as that which is adopted with an indigenous client to the extent that their backgrounds and needs differ. However, few reported that they had adopted special measures to recruit either social workers with these skills or social workers drawn from ethnic minority communities for various reasons which are illustrated in the following responses by 'decision-makers':

"I think one always hopes that one is going to be able to recruit people who have more understanding of the problems of ethnic minorities particularly with respect of the case of children. One attempts to do this but I don't think we specifically advertise in those kind of terms. We have definitely not considered measures to this end and I don't think we are likely to do so. If there was a position being advertised, it would be advertised and we would appoint the best possible applicant for the job; if that applicant happens to be a member of an ethnic minority, then so be it".

"Asian or West Indian clients do not always like to have an Asian or West Indian social workers dealing with them. They don't like to be treated differently. I think it is better to have good training for regularly appointed staff rather than to recruit special staff for immigrant clients".

"It's all very well and fine in theory but once you start embarking on a policy of discriminating among social workers on the grounds of either their colour or the colour of their clients, all sorts of implications come in. I personally believe that we shall get all the ethnic minority social workers we need in the course of time because of the composition of our Borough. That will happen anyway and will improve things".

"I don't think that the general run of our social workers are adequately informed about the cultural background and needs of ethnic minority clients as they are about our indigenous ones".

This concern to be as supportive as possible to ethnic minority groups within an objective professional context was reflected by the social workers as well though they were less cautious about ethnic minority social workers working with ethnic minority clients. Opinion was divided as to whether a common ethnic background was an advantage beyond the initial stages of making contact with a client. In this respect, both ethnic minority and indigenous social workers reported that they were able to draw on each other's background experience in making contact. But a professional commitment was clearly reflected in these interviews as in the following response:

"I'm happy to help. My desire to get involved and also the client's desire to be involved means that I have to watch it. You can't rob a social worker of his or her case. I would only step in if language was very important".

Perhaps understandably, none of the ethnic minority social workers felt that their relations with their indigenous colleagues were affected by their own ethnic origins.

Nevertheless, some social workers deplored the extent to which political caution by local authorities in appointing ethnic minority social workers minimises the impact of the help and support which social workers as a group can give. One said:

"I'd like to see the authority have a much more forward approach in appointing community/social workers from ethnic minority groups".

Another, in a similar vein said:

"There has to be a recognition by the authorities that we all can't be the same. Different ethnic groups have different needs which must be met in different ways".

The issue of the extent to which the training which social workers received is helpful in their tasks evoked some interesting responses. If some 'decision-makers' recognised that more needs to be done in this direction, many of the social workers recognised that their training was inadequate in terms of fitting them for a social work role in a multi-ethnic environment in inner city areas. When asked whether their training had prepared them adequately for their role especially with ethnic minorities, no fewer than 50% of our sample (which contained only 8 ethnic minority social workers) replied that it was inadequate, the most common criticism being that it had not covered problems relating to ethnic minorities or had barely 'touched' on them:

"Not a lot is taught on these courses about the different attitudes of minority groups"

"It didn't enter my professional training and I don't consider that social work training is adequate to cope with even the demands of the host community".

"Empirically it was good but one finds when dealing with the reality of the work that there is so much that is not covered which one needs to know".

When asked further whether the basic work methods adopted by social workers may have changed to help ethnic minority clients, the general feeling was that it had not:

"I don't think we have — although I think we should do. One always questions the conventional approach to ethnic minorities. We try to avoid recognising publicly that they are different. We should look at other ways of dealing with it — study the different cultures and take them into account''.

"Family structures are all different and social workers have to understand the cultural patterns to fit in with them''.

Similar results were obtained by Jones[12] in a study of the response of social services departments to the presence of New Commonwealth immigrants in thirteen multi-racial areas. She found only nine social services departments which offered some sort of special briefing or training for their social workers to enable them to cope with the problems of New Commonwealth immigrant clients. Four of these referred their staff to courses available at local technical colleges or colleges of further education; three referred their staff to courses arranged by the London Boroughs Training committee; two referred their staff to briefing sessions arranged by the local CRC; four mentioned internal briefing; one sent an assistant social worker on a full-time course for immigrant liaison officers, and one planned to send two Senior staff to the West Indies.[13] In the authorities which made no training arrangements, the need for such training or briefing was recognised nevertheless but not acted upon because of shortage of time or resources. This was reflected in the discussions with policy-makers in the course of this survey. For example, one authority recognised that difficulties have arisen for social workers because of the lack of a body of knowledge on matters such as marriage, religious custom and legal situations in ethnic minority communities, but no training had been provided on this. This was because it was felt that social workers already have far too great a range of problems to deal with, "They can't know enough about everything, and they can't be fully proficient in the total range''.

Training for social workers on working with ethnic minority communities at present is almost entirely by means of short courses, catering for a variety of professionals of whom social workers form a part (and often a small part). This means that only a minority of keen social workers attend such courses, which are seen as being of "special interest''. Occasional one-day or weekend conferences may be arranged for social workers by, for example, community relations councils. In this way, perhaps 5-10% of social workers obtain some "briefing'' on ethnic minority communities.

Summary

This examination of the relationship between the needs of ethnic minorities and the perspectives of social workers has not enabled us to quantify the extent of unmet need, nor the extent to which this is the result of inappropriate demands being made on the social services. This failure to quantify reflects the selective nature of social services, with provisions being directed only to the disadvantaged. Decisions about who qualifies for social services inevitably reflect the values of society generally and the values of professional social workers; if the needs of any group of individuals are not met, this is probably because of the low priority placed on their needs as compared with the needs of other groups. For example, one authority we visited said that the need for social work support of all groups in society were neglected or insufficiently met, due to the pressure of meeting the life and death needs of the elderly. There is little evidence to suggest that a very high priority is placed by social services on the needs of ethnic minority communities, and part of their social disadvantage may well arise from their inability to make use of services providing for disadvantaged groups to an extent equal to the rest of the population. An example of this is the study of one-parent families in Haringey, which found that coloured families knew less about, and claimed fewer of the various grants and provisions made for unsupported and low-income families, than the rest of the population.

In sum, there are four major needs of ethnic minority communities for social work assistance in order to alleviate the difficulties they face.

First, is the need for day care facilities, since financial pressures on the family often lead to the need for mothers to work if the family is to be able to stay together as a coping unit.

Second, there is the need for family support services in order to assist families in crisis situations. As has been shown above, ethnic minority families have special difficulties in building sufficient reserves to withstand crisis situations.

Third, there is the need for considerable information about welfare rights, since low incomes account for much of the vulnerability of ethnic minority families. Moreover, ethnic minority families are very proud and resistant to receiving charity, so that care needs to be taken to inform them about their rights in ways which are likely to encourage them to claim welfare facilities as of right.

Fourthly, there is need for much more information among the ethnic minority communities about social work as a profession and the legal powers held by social workers — e.g. their powers to take children into care, or to commit people for mental health treatment. It is difficult for people to understand why a social worker refuses to intervene in some situations where the client expects strong action to be taken, and yet on other occasions exercises his or her legal right to intervene despite the wishes of all concerned. Unless efforts are taken to explain the role of social workers to ethnic minority clients, they are likely to interpret such professional behaviour as further examples of white society discriminating against them.

Chapter Seven: Conclusions

General Conclusions

Our analysis of the relative disadvantages of blacks compared to whites in inner urban areas has demonstrated that there are some needs which are common and other needs which are specific. The Government's approach to urban deprivation as highlighted in the White Paper on the Educational Needs of Immigrants, the White Paper on Racial Discrimination, the White Paper on Race Relations and Housing and the White Paper on Inner Cities, has been based on the assumption that ethnic minorities share the same range of needs with their indigenous counterparts in inner urban areas and that a common provision of services for these areas is likely to meet the needs of both communities. Where it has acknowledged the possibility of specific needs of ethnic minority communities, it has perceived this in the racial discrimination which ethnic minorities experience and in their need for language facilities and information about public services in various ethnic minority languages.

Our findings in this study have demonstrated that this approach is not, in the main, without justification since there are needs which are peculiar to inner city areas because of their physical characteristics as towns with declining employment opportunities, with old industries, with generally dilapidated housing and with a deficit of amenities such as parks and play areas for children. These common needs impinge on ethnic minority communities and indigenous people alike to the extent that they live in these areas. Consequently, population changes within these areas would not significantly reduce these needs. Largely for this reason, inner city areas will continue to require policies and resources which are adequate for tackling the housing, employment, educational and youth problems which exist in these areas, policies which discriminate in favour of these areas and which ensure that people living in the better situated areas and in the rural areas share the burden of dealing with these policies.

However, there are three kinds of difficulties in this approach which deserve serious consideration on the basis of our discussion in this volume. The first difficulty is that this approach considerably over-simplfies the range of needs of people living in inner city areas. Not all the needs of those who live in these areas is due to the physical characteristics of the places in which they are situated. The needs of the elderly, for example, are relevant to indigenous people who constitute by far the majority of those who are retired. Elderly people from ethnic minority groups are not only few and far between but many of them rely on and are able to make use of their community resources to meet their needs. The need for child-care facilities is greater among ethnic minority communities in these areas because of their demographic structure and the long hours they have to spend at work. Similarly, the need for employment opportunities for women in particular is greatest among ethnic minority females since their activity rates are unrelated to the number of dependent children they have to care for. Similarly, the need for language instruction is clearly confined to ethnic minority groups and to Asians (and specifically Pakistani females) in general.

Secondly, a rigid adherence to a 'common provision' approach to areas of urban deprivation presumes that issues like racial discrimination and language instruction are somewhat extraneous to the conditions of life which people in inner city areas experience and can be dealt with by facilitating access to the courts of law in the case of racial discrimination and local provision for language instruction rather than specific local and central government provision of services directed towards these needs. Our findings demonstrate that even in situations in which people in general are disadvantaged, the disadvantages experienced by ethnic minority communities are compounded and are thus transformed into very real obstacles to their welfare. This is clearly brought out in our analysis of employment and housing — two areas in which discrimination has had a lasting effect.

In the case of employment, there has been virtually no change in the socio-economic conditions and location of black people over the past two decades largely because racial discrimination constitutes a barrier between skilled manual occupations and white collar ones even in the case of those who are qualified and experienced. It is, of course, unlikely that the over-representation of ethnic minority workers in the lower rungs of the industrial hiararchy can be expected to disappear overnight even if racial discrimination in employment did not operate in this way or, indeed, did not exist. But given the desire for progress and given the length of time that ethnic minority workers have formed part of the industrial labour force in the country, it is astounding that so little progress has been made by these workers. Similarly, the gross earnings of these workers, earned by working long hours (on permanent night shifts) has restricted them to the lower end of the housing profile even when public housing is taken into account. Yet even in the area of public housing, they experience disadvantages over and above those which their disadvantaged and indigenous counterparts experience. To the extent that there is an association between having language difficulties and the tendency to work permanent night shifts and to the extent that racial discrimination has such a potent effect on promotion opportunities, future earnings potential, access to jobs and access to decent housing, the disadvantages of ethnic minority groups are compounded and transformed into obstacles which their indigenous counterparts do not experience. Racial discrimination and language difficulties are not therefore the extraneous elements that Government's approach may have supposed that they are and while the visible expression of the former is likely to be reduced by the provisions of the Race Relations Act (1976), its subtle interpenetration into various areas of need is unlikely to be significantly affected unless radical administrative measures are adopted at the same time.

Thirdly, the 'common provision' approach is likely to confuse those needs which arise from the newness of ethnic minority communities with those needs which are specific to ethnic minorities in the inner city areas such as those needs that arise from their cultural background and religion. Whereas the former can be expected to disappear in time (e.g. the problem of gaining access to public housings) the latter cannot be expected to disappear anymore than the culture and religion of Judaism among early Jewish immigrants in the East End could have been expected to disappear in time. Indeed, if integration as used by Roy Jenkins is not to be construed as a uniform flattening process, then it is unthinkable that the time will ever come when the cultural and religious backgrounds of ethnic minority groups or, for that matter, Ukranian and Polish immigrants after the War, will disappear. If this is so, then considerable thought ought to be given to those needs which arise from the cultural and religious backgrounds of ethnic minority groups. Official bodies should consider what this would mean for education in particular in view of the fact that many parents from ethnic minority groups would like their children to learn more about their cultural and religious background.

Implications for Inner City and Community Relations Policy

In the light of these considerations, the implications of our findings are three-fold. Firstly, urban deprivation is analytically separate from issues concerning racial discrimination and community relations. However, the two are interrelated in practice insofar as ethnic minority communities constitute part of the population in the conurbations which is exposed to the disadvantages of poor physical environments, inadequate housing, high levels of unemployment and so on. In other words, what we have called the "geography of urban despair" incorporates the majority of the ethnic minority communities in the country. Any discussion therefore about policies for regenerating the inner city which ignores the very visible presence of these communities must therefore be considered to be incomplete. For the same reason, the efforts which are made to regenerate the inner city must provide for the involvement of these communities either in association with the local authorities and voluntary groups in the areas in which they reside or in the form of an encouragement of self-help activities irrespective of how these are administratively organised.

Secondly, financial and other resources for the support of local authorities in areas of urban deprivation must not only be adequate in terms of the nationally available resources but they must also be channelled in such a way that local authorities are helped to assess the needs of residents in their areas, indigenous as well as ethnic minorities, and establish realistic priorities in the light of those needs. The considerable criticisms expressed by the 'decision-makers' who participated in this project concerning the way in which the Urban Programme is administered requires considerable thought in the context of the regeneration of the quality of life in the inner city for they clearly indicate that while the actual physical size of the funds available to the Programme is important, its administration in local authority areas is just as important. Indeed, it is remarkable that many of the 'decision-makers' we interviewed, while recognising the paucity of funds provided under this Programme in the past, nevertheless directed the butt of their criticisms against the way it is administered.

In this regard, the shift of focus in government policies towards the inner city which was central to the Government's White Paper on the Inner City published in 1977[1], is clearly in the right direction insofar as:

(a)   it recognises the crucial role which local authorities must play in the regeneration of the inner city;

(b)   it recognises that other agencies such as voluntary bodies in local areas also have a role to play in partnership with local authorities;

(c)   it recognises that the problems of the inner city can only be handled by a coordinated and unified approach based on a partnership between local authorities and the central government;

(d)   it incorporates a mechanism (in the form of partnership committees) for continuous assessment of local needs in urban areas, the need for which was clearly stressed by the Inner Area Studies as well as by the experimental Comprehensive Community Programmes of the Home Office;

(e)   provides for a shift of emphasis in the main programme areas such as Housing, Education, Social Services etc. towards supporting inner city areas as well as for construction work;

(f)   it expands the Urban Programme from £30 millions to £125 millions by 1979/80 as well as extend its scope to cover environmental projects;

(g)   adopts a policy of positive discrimination to urban areas with social need.

It is too early to assess the extent to which these essentially administrative measures are likely to result in the improvement of the inner city.

However, they are not as radical as they may have been supposed to be when seen in the light of our findings above for several reasons:

(i)   the ethnic minority dimension to urban deprivation is reflected in these proposals only *en passant* insofar as they suggest that partnership committees will take the "pulse" of ethnic minority groups in urban areas; however, they do not include machinery for doing so at central government level, local government level or, indeed, in the partnership committees;

(ii)   the White Paper on Racial discrimination, 1975, emphasised the need for a coordinated approach to community relations matters, an element of which is the law against racial discrimination as embodied in the Race Relations Act 1976; the White Paper on Inner City policy provides for a unified approach to the regeneration of the inner cities in which ethnic minority residents live; however, it does not suggest that this unified approach will be extended to community relations especially in the light of the fact that ethnic minorities live in areas of urban deprivation. It could, of course, be argued that the two issues should have been kept distinct and that issues pertaining to community relations could not have been more fully reflected in the White Paper on Inner City Policy; nevertheless, to ignore the ethnic minority dimension in urban deprivation is to throw the baby out with the bathwater;

(iii) the administrative difficulties about the Urban Programme to which our 'decision-makers' made strong reference remain unaffected by the proposals in the White Paper on Inner City Policy; a mere transfer of the Urban Programme from the Home Office to the Department of the Environment or an expansion of its size is unlikely to improve these difficulties;

(iv) the expansion of the size of the Programme will be welcome by many local authorities; however, the proposals appear to subscribe to the 'hypodermic' assumption that the injection of additional funds into urban areas will necessarily result in the improvement of the conditions of life of urban residents; clearly some improvement will occur; however, there are various 'filter factors' concerned with the approach of local authorities to the services for which they are responsible and the identification of the relative needs of ethnic minority and indigenous residents, which require some consideration; 'rolling monitoring' should contribute towards ensuring that ethnic minority residents in these areas benefit from the additional resources injected into them to the extent that the mechanisms for such monitoring are designed in such a way that they can identify those needs of ethnic minority communities which are due to their newness and which set them apart from their indigenous co-residents as well as those needs which are special to them. The White Paper on Inner City policy did not specify these mechanisms. However, it will be necessary to ensure that such mechanisms are provided for by the partnership committees.

The third implication of our finding is that there are some needs which are common to all urban residents, both indigenous and ethnic minority communities, and some which are separate and distinct and that local authorities can set an example for other agencies in the private sector to follow by:

(a) adapting common services to ensure that these services appeal to ethnic minority communities — the principle inherent in 'curry-on-wheels' in homes for the elderly is an example of how such adaptation could be effected. It also requires the provision of housing aid advice, information on rate and rent rebates, improvement grants, mortgage conditions, public health legislation etc. in the languages of ethnic minority groups. Information on the Social Services Departments and their legal obligations also has to be presented in a similar way;

(b) local authorities could also usefully provide for priority to be given to ethnic minority groups in those categories of need in which they predominate e.g. child care, homelessness etc. since some ethnic minority groups predominate among both categories of need;

(c) local authorities are sensitive to the issue of providing special services to meet the special needs of ethnic minorities. Nevertheless, where there are distinct needs arising from specific problems such as language facilities or the accummulated result of racial discrimination, then specific measures and specific services should be considered to meet these needs. The language needs of ethnic minority pupils in school have so far received this treatment (though our finding that only 10% of our laymen reported that their children had received such language instruction is surprising).

To be sure, our survey of policy-makers revealed a distinct avoidance of matters pertaining to the provision of specific services for ethnic minorities partly because it was felt that this would amount to racial discrimination in reverse and partly because of the political and other repercussions which such a consideration might give rise to. Consequently, a number of 'decision-makers' were opposed to exploring the very concept of special needs. The PEP, it will be recalled, also found a similar tendency among 'decision-makers' (in their study of housing) to think that their housing policies are based on 'housing need'. There is clearly a considerable degree of sensitivity — 'a chip on their shoulders' (to use a well-known phrase) — among 'decision-makers' which has so far prevented them from examining their services from this point of view and, indeed, the concept of racial discrimination itself. Even those concerned with services that are based on discrimination according to the severity of needs (e.g. social services) disclaimed a concern with the concept of 'discrimination' because of this sensitivity. Yet, there were a few 'decision-makers' (elected councillors) whose thought processes had penetrated beyond the word 'racial discrimination' and who recognised the need for some distinct services for ethnic minorities especially in the social services but who felt free to discuss it with their colleagues only outside of the Council Chamber. They also recognised that the distinction between adaptations of common services and distinct services for ethnic minorities can merge into each other in some circumstances e.g. curry-on-wheels in Old People's Homes with retired ethnic minority people. Clearly, a major de-sensitising exercise will be required to enable 'decision-makers' to locate 'racial discrimination' within its proper context and to recognise that the entire welfare state system is based on an ability to discriminate between need categories — those who need unemployment benefit as against those who do not, those who are well off as against those who are not and those who need social services against those who do not.

Appendix 1: Methodology

Terms of Reference

The terms of reference of this inquiry were:

"To consider the extent to which the needs of ethnic minority communities differ from those of the rest of the population in areas of urban deprivation; to report; and to advise on the implications for community relations policy;"

The operative concepts in these terms of reference are *areas of urban deprivation*, the *needs of ethnic minority* communities and the *needs of indigenous people* living in these areas.

Our overall approach to urban deprivation was based on the need to recognise the interpenetration of the structural characteristics of inner city areas and the 'welfare' characteristics. By structural characteristics, we refer to problems concerning housing, employment and education and by 'welfare' characteristics, we refer to problems concerning the availability or non-availability of the social and income-maintaining services (rates and rent rebates, supplementary benefits etc.) as well as the extent to which the content and style of presentation of these services contribute towards meeting the needs of both ethnic minority communities and indigenous people. By adopting this approach to urban deprivation, we were able to explore the extent to which problems within the structural sphere — housing, employment, education — contribute to, and reinforce, problems within the welfare sphere including the extent to which residents are aware of such welfare facilities as are available.

From the inception of this project, we recognised that a strict interpretation of the operative concepts in the terms of reference would require us to investigate not only the range of problems we have outlined above but also other problems such as juvenile delinquency in urban areas, police/immigrant relations, the operation of estate agents, the availability of solicitors' services in these areas and so on. Such an extensive interpretation would have widened the project beyond our human resources and would have minimised the impact of the exercise since it would have been difficult, if not impossible, to cover each area with the thoroughness which it deserves.

It was therefore decided at the initial stages of this project to concentrate on a few aspects of life in areas of urban deprivation and to draw on published material and on-going work to illustrate issues which impinge on our inquiry but which could not be dealt with in depth.

It was largely for this reason that we decided to focus the project on those services which impinge rather directly on the lives of those who live in areas of urban deprivation. These services are mainly administered by local authorities, who are also responsible for determining such policies as should apply to the communities who live within their areas. Central government responsibility for the quality of life of people who live in these areas is not thereby minimised since it provides an important lead for the policies which are adopted within local areas by local authorities. Understandably, therefore our findings and our recommendations do not apply only to local authorities but also to central government agencies and departments. It was in this way that we were able to give specific meaning, in the context of local areas, to the concept of *needs* both in relation to ethnic minority communities and in relation to the indigenous people who live in the inner city areas.

Selection of Project Areas

The project areas were selected on the basis of statistical information provided by the 1971 Population Census so as to yield a representative spread of areas of urban deprivation in the North, Midlands, South and London regions of the country.

Further, a number of criteria were set up as guides for the selection of project areas. To be selected, project areas had to:
1. Contain mixed populations of ethnic minorities and indigenous people,
2. Contain a population in excess of 200,000,
3. Contain a mixture of ethnic minority groups from New Commonwealth,
4. by most of the accepted criteria, be judged by professionals in the area to contain at least two wards which have a severe incidence of urban deprivation.

According to these criteria, the following areas were those initially identified:

Ealing, Hackney, Haringey, Slough, Bristol, Leicester, Wolverhampton, Manchester, Liverpool and Bradford. However, Liverpool and Wolverhampton were excluded from the list for various reasons. The population characteristics of the remaining eight were as follows:

Region	Towns	Total Population	New Commw. Population	NC born as % of total
North	Manchester	543,650	17,290	3.18
	Bradford	461,785	22,815	4.94
Midlands	Leicester	284,210	23,280	8.20
South	Bristol	426,655	8,775	2.06
London (Outer)	Haringey	240,080	34,595	14.41
	Ealing	301,110	33,440	11.11
	Slough	99,515	8,710	8.76
London (Inner)	Hackney	220,280	25,455	11.56

Within each area, two or three inner city neighbourhoods were selected as the foci for fieldwork which were judged by senior officials of the local authority to be deprived in terms of their housing, educational, employment and physical characteristics. In some cases these areas corresponded to electoral wards, in other cases to enumeration districts and in some cases were simply acknowledged as areas of great stress which did not relate to any official boundary designations. The classic example of this is the "Finsbury Park Triangle" in Haringey.

Sampling Procedure

In conducting research on many aspects of social behaviour, it is critical to the validity of the data to ensure that all individuals in specified areas have a calculable probability of being selected. The normal sampling procedure is to use the Electoral Register as a sampling frame. In this instance, this course of action was rejected for three reasons:

i)   In areas of high mobility many respondents will not be recorded on the Electoral Register.

ii)   While such non-electors can be sampled by allowing for a procedure to select non-electors in elector households, many households, will not be represented at all.

iii) The high incidence of multi-household dwellings can in itself invalidate non-elector selection within elector households.

As a solution to this problem it was decided that a random walk technique should be applied. This involved Opinion Research Centre executives (who assisted with the fieldwork) preparing maps of the designated area before fieldwork and randomly selecting a starting address. Interviewers were then required to call at this address and at a specified interval of addresses thereafter (normally ever fifth or sixth). Every person living at the dwelliing was then listed and one individual selected for interview according to a standard grid reference of random numbers. An additional quota control was implemented to ensure that too great a preponderance of white respondents was not selected in the overall sample, ie supervisors were instructed that if a specified number of white respondents had been interviewed in each area, they should then reject listed white respondents and continue to make up their full quota with respondents from ethnic minority groups. In practice, it was seldom necessary to implement this procedure.

Selection of 'Decision-makers' and Professional Practitioners
The random walk technique described above was applied to the selection of the lay persons sample and not to the selection of the 'decision-makers' and professional practitioners' samples. With regards to the 'decision-makers', consultations with Chief Executives indicated the range of likely interest within their local authorities; and all the relevant senior officials and elected Chairmen of the relevant Committees were approached and invited to participate in the interviews. Since our interest in these interviews was with the policies which are adopted and with the way these policies are formulated, we interviewed every senior official (and Committee Chairman) who agreed to participate. It was therefore not necessary to collect background details of these officers (other than their existing roles).

Virtually the same procedure was adopted with the professional practitioners and for virtually the same reasons though we were also anxious to find out whether responses differed according to the racial background of the respondent. In the event, we drew up lists of professional practitioners operating within the project areas and selected for interview those who were willing to participate; overall, there were few ethnic minority professionals within our practitioner sample. The composition of this sample was as follows:

Teachers (Primary, Middle & Secondary Schools)	46
Social Workers	48
Playgroup Leaders	21
Home Help Organisers	10
Advice Centre Staff	5
Community Centre Wardens	6
Matrons of Day Nurseries	15
Detached Youth Workers	12
Youth Club Workers	32
Total Sample	195

Interview schedules

A number of questionnaires were designed to cover (a) each subject area of interest for the project and (b) each 'level' of respondents as follows:

	Housing	Education	Social Services	Youth
'Decision-makers'	1	1	1	1
Professional				
Practitioners		1	1	1
Lay Persons		1	1	1

It will be recalled that no interviews were conducted in the field of employment for reasons which have been outlined in the main body of this work. Similarly, housing was not explored in detail partly because a mass of secondary material was already available from work undertaken by the Community Relations Commission and partly because the Survey of racial Minorities to which we referred earlier (PEP) had produced relevant background material. In sum, ten questionnaires were used in the surveys.

A limited number of pilot interviews were carried out and it was agreed that the Bradford area should serve as a pilot area.

Fieldwork — Lay Persons Interviews

The interviewing was carried out on a team basis. Interviewers had been selected and trained before the survey started and an attempt was made to relate interviewers fluent in particular languages or of particular ethnic origins to the areas in which respondents of that group were likely to be found. In practice we endeavoured to place West Indian interviewers in West Indian areas, Greek Cypriots in Greek Cypriot areas, Punjabi speaking Asians in Punjabi speaking areas etc.

Each team of interviewers consisted of three people, one of whom was either a supervisor or an assistant supervisor. At all times the team worked together and this allowed for a very high level of supervisory control during fieldwork.

Almost 30% of all the interviews were carried out in the presence of a supervisor or an assistant supervisor. In addition, the supervisor was able to do 'on the spot' checks of respondents and interviewers. This was a much higher level of control than would normally be used, but it was thought necessary because of:

(a) the relative inexperience of some of the interviewers; and

(b) the probable inadequacy of normal methods of postal backchecking.

In this way, a total of 1,403 lay persons were interviewed and were made up of 298 white British, 320 West Indians, 123 Cypriots, 30 Africans, 314 Indians, 190 Pakistanis, 75 East African Asians, 15 Bangladeshis, 15 other Asians and

23 other ethnic minority members. It also involved 195 professional practitioners and 86 decision-makers, making up a total of 1,684 respondents.

'Decision-Makers' and Practitioners Interviews

The interviews with 'decision-makers' were in-depth interviews and lasted for an average of one hour. Invariably, the interviews with 'decision-makers' in the Social Services lasted much longer. By contrast, the interviews with lay persons and professional practitioners were much shorter and lasted for an average of forty-five minutes. It is indeed, a tribute to the patience of all interviewees and the enthusiasm with which they welcomed our discussions, that we were able to undertake such wide-ranging interviews with so many different categories of interviewees. Many of the 'decision-makers' welcomed the project because it provided an opportunity for them to think through the various policies which they had adopted in their local areas to the rationale which should inform general thinking on urban deprivation and ethnic minorities at a national level. Many also welcomed the opportunity of comparing the success which they had achieved in their local areas with that which had been achieved in other areas where similar policies had been adopted.

Administration and Control

The inquiry was undertaken by Dr. C. P. Cross. It was supported by an Advisory Steering Committee composed of officers from various divisions within the Community Relations Commisions, Community Relations Officers drawn from the field and other persons with expertise in community relations work.

Members of the Advisory Steering Committee were:

Mr. Charan Rai — Hillingdon Community Relations Council
Miss Sarah Berry — Northampton Community Relations Council
Mr. George Greaves — Lambeth Community Relations Council
Miss Kate Francis — National Association of Community Relations
    Councils
Mr. Malcolm Lawrence — National Association of Community Relations
    Councils
Miss Anna Schiff — Development Division, Community Relations
    Commission

We are grateful to them for their advice and co-operation and to Dr. Ken Pryce for his assistance with the planning and initial consultations which we undertook.

Consultations
Extensive consultations were held on this inquiry with various organisations. We consulted the Association of District Councils, the Association of Metropolitan Authorities, the London Boroughs Association, the Association of County Councils, the Greater London Council, the Inner London Education Authority, the Home Office Urban Deprivation Unit, the National Association of Community Relations Councils, the Association of Scientific, Technical and Managerial Staffs as well as national organisations of immigrants — the Standing Conference of West Indian Organisations, the Standing Conference of Indian Organisations, the Standing Conference of Pakistani Organisations, the Greek Cypriot Parents' Association and The Office of the Turkish Cypriot Administration in London.

Further, five regional consultations with community relations officers from various areas were held in Leeds, in Birmingham and in London respectively.

A further round of consultations was held with senior officials of local authorities in the areas in which the project was conducted.

Operational Phasing
The inquiry was carried out in four phases. The first phase involved the preliminary planning of the project in consultation with various divisions within the Community Relations Commission. It also included the extensive consultations which we held with various national organisations as well as with community relations officers and immigrant organisations. The second phase consisted of discussions with the Chief Executives and other senior officials of the various local authorities, to inform them of the nature of the project and to explore the neighbourhoods/wards within their areas which were to be selected for undertaking the interviews. The third phase consisted of the fieldwork interviews with lay persons, professional practitioners and policy 'decision-makers' in the various local authorities in the project areas. The fourth and final phase consisted of the analysis of the data obtained in the interviews and the writing up of the final report.

Appendix 2: Additional Tables

TABLE 1: Over- Or Under-representation* of Different Immigrant Groups in different occupations, 1966.

(a)   MALES — GREATER LONDON CONURBATION

Occupation	India	Pakistan	Jamaica	Rest of Caribbean	All Caribbean	British West Africa	Cyprus
VIII Woodworkers			+	+	+		
XI Clothing Workers		+					+
XVIII Labourers			+ +	+	+ +		
XIX Transport and communications workers				+	+		−
XXI Clerical workers	+		−	−	−	+ +	−
XXII Sales workers			−	−	−	−	
XXIII Service, sport and recreation workers		+					+ + +
XXIV Administrators and managers			−	−	−		
XXV Professional, technical workers, artists	+		−	−	−	+	−

(b) MALES — WEST MIDLANDS CONURBATIONS

	India	Pakistan	Jamaica	All Caribbean
V Furnace, forge, foundry, rolling mill workers	+ +			
VII Engineering and allied trades workers	−	−		
XVIII Labourers				
110. Labourers in engineering and allied trades	+	+ + +	+	+
XIX Transport and communications workers		+		
XXI Clerical workers			−	
XXIII Sales workers		−	−	−
XXV Professional, technical workers, artists		−	−	−

Notes for Tables 1 (a) and 1(b)
*Over- or under-representation is the difference between the percentage of those in employment for the immigrant group in question in a particular occupation and the percentage of the total population in the same occupation. Only differences of 5% or more are shown and plus (+) denotes over-representation, minus (−) under-representation of the immigrant group in comparison to the total population.

+ or −	Difference between 5% and 9.9% inclusive
+ + or − −	Difference between 10% and 19.9% inclusive
+ + + or − − −	Difference between 10% and 34.9% inclusive
+ + + + or − − − −	Difference between 35% and 49.9% inclusive

Source: 1966 10% Sample Census and EJB Rose op. cit. pp. 168-9.

TABLE 2

MALES — JOB LEVEL ANALYSED BY COUNTRY OF ORIGIN

Men in Job Market Who Have Worked	White	West Indian	Pakistani/ Bangladeshis	Indian	African/ Asian
(unweighted)	996	634	495	508	226
(weighted)	1594	2896	1391	1867	1050
Job level (socio-economic group):	%	%	%	%	%
Professional/ Management	23))40	2)) 8	4)) 8	8))20	10))30
White collar	17)	6)	4)	12)	20)
Skilled manual	42	59	33	44	44
Semi-skilled manual	12))18	23) 32)	38))58	27))36	24))26
Unskilled manual	6)	9)	20)	9)	2)
Not classified	1	1	1	*	*

Source: PEP Survey of Racial Minorities op.cit. p.110.

*no responses in these categories.

TABLE 3a: Industrial Status of Those in Employment for Selected Birthplace Groups, by Percentage, by Sex 1966

MALES — GREATER LONDON CONURBATION

	India	Pakistan	Jamaica	Rest of Caribbean	All Caribbean	British West Africa	Cyprus	Total Population
Number in employment*	35,470	9,140	32,400	29,340	61,740	7,940	17,940	2,410,420
Self-employed	3.7	6.0	1.5	1.2	1.4	0.9	19.6	7.1
Managers, foremen and supervisors	8.3	4.4	1.1	2.7	1.9	2.9	5.9	15.3
Apprentices, articled clerks and formal trainees	4.2	4.7	1.9	2.5	2.2	7.9	3.2	4.1
Professional employees	8.2	4.2	0.4	1.2	0.8	5.7	1.7	4.2
Other employees	75.6	80.7	95.1	92.4	93.7	82.6	69.6	69.3

*Figures for the number in employment have been multiplied by ten, as the size of the sample was 10% of the total population.

Source: 1966 10% Sample Census and EJB Rose op. cit. pp. 154.

TABLE 3b: Industrial Status of Those in Employment for Selected Birthplace Groups, by Percentage, by Sex 1966

MALES — WEST MIDLANDS CONURBATIONS

	India	Pakistan	Jamaica	Rest of Caribbean	All Caribbean	Total Pop-ulation
Number in employment*	12,450	11,170	13,050	3,290	16,340	763,610
Self-employed	2.9	1.98	0.8	1.5	0.9	4.5
Managers, foremen and supervisors	2.2	0.7	0.3	0.9	0.4	12.3
Apprentices, articled clerks and formal trainees	2.9	0.3	1.8	3.3	2.1	4.8
Professional employees	2.6	0.3	0.2	0.3	0.2	3.0
Other employees	89.4	97.0	96.9	94.0	96.4	75.4

* Figures for the number in employment have been multiplied by ten, as the size of the sample was 10% of the total population.

Source: 1966 10% Sample Census and EJB Rose ibid. p. 154.

TABLE 4: Percentage Socio-economic Distribution* for Different Immigrant Groups Selected Areas, 1966

(a) MALES — SELECTED LONDON BOROUGHS 1966

	Jamaica	Rest of Caribbean	All Caribbean	Ireland	England and Wales
Number economically active	12,070	8,340	20,500	14,400	206,750
1 Professional workers	0.4	0.4	0.4	1.0	3.1
2 Employers and managers	0.3	0.3	0.3	3.6	8.3
3 Non-manual	2.3	7.8	4.6	13.2	22.1
4 Skilled manual and foremen	42.8	37.2	40.5	36.5	39.6
5 Semi-skilled manual	24.1	30.5	26.7	19.7	15.7
6 Unskilled manual	27.0	22.4	25.1	24.8	9.9
7 Armed Forces and inadequately described	3.1	1.4	2.4	1.2	1.3

(b) FEMALES — SELECTED LONGON BOROUGHS, 1966

	Jamaica	Rest of Caribbean	All Caribbean	Ireland	England and Wales
Number economically active	8,450	5,500	13,950	8,500	146,820
1 Professional workers	—	0.2	0.1	0.4	0.8
2 Employers and managers	0.1	—	0.1	2.3	3.7
3 Non-manual	19.4	23.6	21.1	36.8	50.6
4 Skilled manual	8.7	9.7	9.1	5.6	8.5
5 Semi-skilled manual	60.0	53.1	57.3	38.9	24.4
6 Unskilled manual	8.8	11.5	9.8	14.9	11.0
7 Armed Forces and inadequately described	3.0	1.9	2.5	1.1	1.0

(c) MALES — SELECTED WEST MIDLANDS WARDS, 1966

	Indian	Pakistan	Jamaica	All Caribbean	Ireland	England and Wales
Number economically active	8,260	8,860	10,190	12,840	13,190	138,740
1 Professional workers	1.4	—	0.3	0.4	1.5	3.0
2 Employers and managers	1.0	1.1	—	—	2.4	7.0
3 Non-manual	3.5	2.0	2.1	1.7	5.6	14.2
4 Skilled manual and foremen	41.5	15.5	46.3	46.1	40.2	47.0
5 Semi-skilled manual	20.4	24.4	27.3	26.2	26.0	19.9
6 Unskilled manual	30.1	55.1	21.7	22.2	23.3	7.7
7 Armed Forces and inadequately described	2.1	1.9	2.3	3.4	1.0	1.2

(d)   FEMALES — SELECTED WEST MIDLANDS WARDS, 1966

	Jamaica	All Caribbean	Ireland	England And Wales
Number economically active + +	5,920	7,470	5,450	91,110
1 Professional workers	—	—	0.7	0.4
2 Employers and managers	—	—	2.2	3.1
3 Non-manual	17.1	17.8	20.4	38.6
4 Skilled manual	14.2	14.6	8.7	12.1
5 Semi-skilled manual	55.5	55.1	53.4	35.1
6 Unskilled manual	8.3	8.0	11.7	10.1
7 Armed Forces and inadequately described	4.9	4.5	2.9	0.6

Key to Tables 4 (a), (b), (c) and (d)

*Categories used in tables consist of the following:

1. Professional workers, Registrar-General's S.E.G., 3,4.
2. Employers and managers, Registrar-General's S.E.G., 1,2,13.
3. Non-manual, Registrar-General's S.E.G., 5,6.
4. Skilled manual, Registrar-General's S.E.G., 8,9,12,14.
5. Semi-skilled manual, Registrar-General's S.E.G., 7,10,15.
6. Unskilled manual, Registrar-General's S.E.G., 11.
7. Armed Forces and inadequately described, Registrar-General's S.E.G., 16,17.

+ + Figures for the number economically active have been multiplied by ten as the size of the sample was 10% of the total population.

Source: 1966 10% Sample Census and EJB Rose op. cit. pp. 173-5.

Appendix 3: Profiles of Laymen and Professional Practitioners

LAYMEN SAMPLE
Ethnic Language and Religious Groups
The composition of the sample does not reflect exactly the population of the selected areas, since the number of interviews with white British respondents was limited. The distribution of the various ethnic minority groups in the sample, however, reflects the ethnic minority population of the areas since a random sampling procedure was used, with the reservation that in some cases (e.g. Haringey Cypriots) booster samples were taken according to the regular procedure to ensure a sufficiently high data base.

The interviewing districts were selected on an empirical basis and do not necessarily correspond to any administrative or electoral districts. There is thus no data available with which the composition of this sample can be compared.

In each of the eight areas, one or other of the ethnic minority groups predominates. In Haringey 53% of the samples are Cypriot (44% Greek and 6% Turkish speaking). West Indians predominate in Bristol (48%) and in Manchester (40%). Asians from India are the main group in Ealing (51%) and Leicester (42%), and Asians from Pakistan are the main group in Bradford (43%). In Leicester, 25% of respondents are East African Asians and in Slough the majority of respondents are Asian, 38% of Indian origin and 27% from Pakistan. In Hackney the sample is more diverse, the largest group (West Indians) make up just over a third of the respondents.

The majority of respondents in Haringey, Bristol, Hackney and Manchester are Christians. In Bradford 49% are Muslim, in Leicester 49% are Hindu and 33% are Sikh. In Slough, Muslim and Christians each account for 30% of the sample and Sikhs for a further 25%.

In Bristol and Manchester the majority of respondents speak no language other than English. In Hackney just over half have no other language. In Leicester 48% of respondents speak Gujarati, in Slough and in Ealing, Punjabi is the main Asian language group.

Age and Length of Residence in England
Approximately one-quarter of the sample is in each of the three age ranges, 16-24, 25-34 and 35-44. Only 7% are in the ranges 55-64 and over 65. This is a

much younger age profile than in the population of the United Kingdom as a whole, of whom one-third are over 55 and only 16% between 16 and 24.

The white British respondents tend to be rather older than those in the ethnic minority groups. 21% of them are over 65 and only 17% under 25. Cypriots and East African Asians are rather younger, 32% of each group being under 25.

In line with their rather younger age profile, Cypriots are more likely to have been born in the United Kingdom than are members of the other ethnic minority groups. The East African Asians are, of course, most likely to have arrived within the past five years. The West Indians tend to have been in Britain longest, only 10% of those born abroad have been in Britain for less than 10 years.

Occupational Status

53% of the total sample are employed full-time and a further 6% part-time. The proportion is lowest among the white British, 20% of whom are retired. 8% of the sample are unemployed. This is in fact 12% of the 947 respondents who are employable (not students, retired or housewives), a considerably higher proportion than among the population as a whole.

Cypriots are less likely to be unemployed than the other ethnic minority groups. Respondents in Leicester and Bristol are more likely to be unemployed than those in other areas. In Bristol, a higher proportion are employed only part-time than in other areas.

Only 29% of the women in the sample were working full-time compared to 73% of the men; a further 12% of women were working part-time (2% of men). 40% of them were housewives and therefore not working.

PROFESSIONAL PRACTITIONERS

Teachers

The final sample of 46 teachers was drawn from 20 schools in seven areas. The distribution is shown below. The secondary group includes one school which is both middle and secondary. Nursery, infants and junior schools are included in the primary group.

| | | *All* | *Type of School* | | |
			Primary	*Middle*	*Secondary*
Ealing	(Schools)	(3)	—	(3)	—
	Respondents	9		9	
Haringey	(Schools)	(4)	(3)	—	(1)
	Respondents	7	5		2
Bradford	(Schools)	(2)	*(1)	(1)	—
	Respondents	6	3	3	

Slough	(Schools)	(3)	(2)	(1)	—
	Respondents	6	3	3	
Leicester	(Schools)	(2)	(1)	—	(1)
	Respondents	6	3		3
Bristol	(Schools)	(3)	(2)	—	(1)
	Respondents	6	4		2
Manchester	(Schools)	(3)	(2)	—	(1)
	Respondents	6	4		2
TOTAL	(Schools)	(20)	(11)	(5)	(4)
	Respondents	46	22	15	9

*All Infants Centre for Asian children who do not speak English. It has been included with the Primary schools in the report where the questions were relevant to the particular situation there.

In the majority of schools the head teacher was interviewed and in many cases also the deputy. The table below shows the position held by the respondent:

		Type of school		
	All	*Primary*	*Middle*	*Secondary*
Head	19	11	5	3
Deputy Head	11	5	4	2
Senior teacher/				
Head of Department	7	1	3	3
Teacher	9	5	3	1

All but one of the respondents were white British, one was of Chinese origin. All were born in the United Kingdom and trained there, thirteen of them in the locality in which they are now working. The distribution of age and sex is shown below:

		Type of School		
	All	*Primary*	*Middle*	*Secondary*
Sex				
Male	22	6	8	8
Female	24	16	7	1
Age				
16—24	4	1	2	1
25—34	8	3	4	1
35-44	9	5	1	3
45—54	15	8	4	3
55—64	10	5	4	1

Social Workers

Sex and age profile of the sample

Male 27
Female 21

16—24	2
25—34	22
35—44	19
45—54	3
55—64	2
65 +	—
	48

Ethnic origin of the sample

White (born UK)	37
White (born in old Commonwealth)	3
Greek Cypriot	1
West Indian	2
Hong Kong (Chinese)	1
Indian	1
Kenyan Asian	2
Mauritian Asian	1
	48

Residence in UK

2 months, 5 years, 20 years
18 years
10 years, 19 years
10 years
14 years
9 years, 5 years
10 years

Place of training

Locally	22
Elsewhere in UK	17
Locally and elsewhere in UK	3
Outside UK	3
No training	3
	48

Area worked in

Ealing	11
Hackney	6
Haringey	5
Bradford	6
Slough	6
Leicester	5
Leicester	5
Bristol	4
Manchester	5

Job Title

Area Officer	3
Area Leader	2
Social Worker	22
Community Worker	2
Senior Principal/ Social Worker	15
Other	4

Location

Central office	5
Area Office	43

Length of time in job

Under 1 year	11
1 year—3 years	24
3 years—5 years	10
Over 5 years	3

Nature of caseload

None (mainly admin/don't deal with individual cases)	4
Generic caseload	40
Specialist caseload	4
The four specialists: 3 child care, 1 mental health	

Playgroup Leaders

19 of the playgroup leaders were women, two were men. They were all white and, except for one American, were all born in England. They were mostly aged between 25 and 44, the exact distribution being:

	No.
16—24	2
25—34	9
35—44	8
45—54	1
55—64	—
65 +	1

A number of the respondents were 'founder members' of their playgroups. Few of them had been working there for more than five years. The distribution of the length of time worked was:

	No.
Under 1 year	4
1—2 years	5
Over 2—3 years	3
Over 3—4 years	3
Over 4—5 years	2
Over 5—6 years	1
Over 6—7 years	—
Over 7—8 years	2
Over 8—9 years	1

Nine of the playgroups were run by the Council through the Social services or other Departments. Three of them were run by groups of parents, another four by a group of helpers and a further three by a local playgroup association. Two were run by churches.

Three of the playgroups were self-supporting:

"It is a voluntary group — unpaid. To get the climbing frame, large toys etc., we raise funds by mainly jumble sales etc".

Four were currently financed by an Urban aid grant and others were wholly or partly funded by the local Council.

All eight of the survey areas were represented. The interviews were distributed as shown below:—

	No.
Ealing	1
Hackney	3
Haringey	4
Bradford	2
Slough	3
Leicester	3
Bristol	4
Manchester	1

Home-Help Organisers

The ten home-help organisers interviewed were all female and white. Each of the eight interviewing areas was represented; in two areas, Haringey and Bradford, two area home-help organisers were interviewed.

All but one of the respondents had been trained in Britain. The remaining respondent, a deputy home-help organiser had had no training.

All the respondents provided home-help for several hundred families. Five respondents said there was no waiting list, one had no actual list but there were people without home-help. Four had waiting periods of between one and three weeks.

Advice Centre Staff

Three of the advice centre workers were women, two were men. All five were white British.

They had varied backgrounds for the work. Two were former social workers, one was trained as a community worker, one was ex-police and the othe had had some instruction from the Public Health Advisory Service.

Those whose 'training' had included a lot of practical experience thought it adequate preparation, the other did not.

"I don't think it could You learn from experience and every case you take on".

"No — I would have liked some training — of the ethnic religions — which I have tried to do myself. I would like to have known a little of the languages".

The respondents worked in Hackney, Haringey, Bradford, Leicester and Bristol.

Community Centre Wardens

Five of the six community centre wardens were white. One was a black African from Rhodesia. They were all men.

Three of the community centres were run by the Local Authority Education Departments. Two were run by Local Community Associations, with some grant-aid from the Local Authority and one was run by the Salvation Army.

Three of the centres had been in existence for twenty-years or more and three for five years or less. One of the wardens had been there since the centre opened. None of the others had been there more than five years.

The areas represented were in Ealing, Hackney, Slough, Leicester, Bristol and Manchester.

Day Nursery Matrons

The fifteen day nursery matrons interviewed were all women, all white and all trained in England. Their age range was:

	No.
16—24	1
25—34	3
35—44	4
45—54	4
55—64	3

Nine of them had worked in the nurseries for three years or less. Only three had worked there for longer than five years.

The day nurseries were all run by the Social Services Departments of the Local Authority. Six of them had been open for ten years or more (three over 20 years). Five had been open for three years or less.

Youth Club Workers

As many youth club workers as possible were interviewed in each area. The final sample included 32 club workers from 26 clubs in eight areas distributed as shown in the table below:

Youth Club Workers

As many youth club workers as possible were interviewed in each area. The final sample included 32 club workers from 26 clubs in eight areas distributed as shown in the table below:

AREA	Number of Workers	Number of Clubs	All White	Type of Club Mixed	
	2	2	—	2	1
Hackney	4	3	—	2	1
Haringey	5	5	—	2	3
Bradford	6	2	—	2	—
Slough	3	3	—	1	2
Leicester	2	2	1	1	—
Bristol	6	5	1	1	3
Manchester	4	4	—	1	2
TOTAL	32	26	2	12	12

The majority of workers were men and half were aged between 25 and 34. All but eleven where white.

	Number of youth workers
Sex	
Male	28
Female	4
Age	
16—24	3
25—34	16
35—44	7
45—54	5
55—64	1
Ethnic group	
Black (West Indian)	7
Asian	3
Mixed race	1
White	21
Country of Birth	
UK	20
Not UK:	12
West Indies	8
India	3
Eire	1

None of those born abroad had been in Britain for less than five years, nine of them had been here for over ten years. None of the respondents received their training outside of the United Kingdom.

The majority of the clubs were run by local authorities. There was a wide spread in the length of time the clubs had been open.

	Number of clubs
Local Authority-run	18
Other:	8
Police Boys Club	1
YMCA	1
Methodist Church	1
Trust Committee	1
Independent Committee	4

Length of time operating	Number of clubs
1—5 years	9
6—10 years	5
11—15 years	4
16—20 years	3
21—30 years	1
31—40 years	3
41—50 years	1

The length of time that individual workers have been working in their present clubs also varied widely though only two had spent over ten years there.

Time in present club	Number of workers
Under 1 year	2
1—2 years	8
Over 2 — up to 3 years	9
Over 3 — up to 4 years	5
Over 4 — up to 5 years	5
Over 5 — up to 10 years	1
Over 10 — up to 15 years	1
Over 15 — up to 20 years	1

The number of young people using the club varied widely, some clubs were open every night and had a large number of irregular users, some were very small. The estimates of numbers were often only very approximate since no records are kept. The majority of the clubs had more boys than girls, a few were fairly evenly mixed. None had more girls than boys. The majority of workers said that most of the club users were under 16.

"60-80 each night, ranging from 13-24 officially, but youngsters try to pretend they're 13 and older ones that they are only 24".

Only one respondent thought that one of the club users were from disadvantaged backgrounds. Six thought that 30% or less were from such backgrounds, ten that 31%—60% were and 10 that 61%—90% were. Only one worker said that all users of his club were from disadvantaged backgrounds and two that they did not know.

Only one respondent would not consider the breakdown of club users into the various ethnic groups:

"Multi-racial — period. Equally split".

Few respondents could give exact figures.

Detached Youth Workers

Of the twelve respondents seven were white, two Asian and three black (two West Indians, one Nigerian); ten were men, two women (one white and one West Indian). All but two were employed by the Local Authority; one of the others was employed by the Community Relations Commission and one by the Urban Aid Programme and a trust.

Only one of them had been working in the area for longer than three years nd they were all aged between 16 and 44.

Age	No.
16—24	3
25—34	6
35—44	3

Length of Service

Under 6 months	1
6 months—1 year	3
Over 1 year, up to 2	4
Over 2 years up to 3	3
6 years	1

In two of the eight study areas we were unable to find a detached youth worker. The workers were distributed as shown below:

	White	Asian	Black
Ealing	1	1	1
Haringey	1	—	1
Slough	1	—	—
Leicester	3	—	—
Bristol	1	—	1
Manchester	—	1	—

Notes and References

Preface
1. C. P. Cross "Youth Clubs and Coloured Youths" *New Community,* Vol. V. No. 4, 1977 and his "Urban Deprivation and Ethnic Minorities: A Study of the Resource Delivery System in Urban Areas in England" *Human Rights Review,* Vol. 3, 1978 (forthcoming).
2. For the background to the presence of coloured people in England see, Sheila Allen *New Minorities, Old Conflicts: Asian and West Indian Migrants in Britain,* New York: Random House, 1971. Sheila Patterson *Immigration and Race Relations in Britain 1960-1967,* London: OUP, 1969 and Clifford Hill *Immigration and Integration: A Study of the Settlement of Coloured Minorities in Britain,* Oxford: Pergamon Press, 1970.

Chapter 1: Urban Deprivation and Ethnic Minorities in England
1. John Stewart et al. "Local Government and Urban Deprivation", Home Office Deprivation Unit, May 1974, Appendix, Chap. 1.
2. For an analysis of the situation in London, see Graham Lomas *The Inner City,* London Council of Social Services, 1974 esp. chap. 1; for a discussion of these issues on a national basis, see F.J.C. Amos "Inner Cities and Social Priorities", text of a lecture delivered to the Royal Society of Arts, 6th April, 1977.
3. Rt. Hon. Sir Keith Joseph's speech at a Conference for Local Authorities organised by the Pre-School Playgroups Association, Thursday, 29th June, 1972, and his speech to the spring Study Seminar on the Cycle of Deprivation to the Association of Directors of Social Services, Brighton, 1973, March.
4. Ibid. p.5.
5. Social Science Research Council, Working Party on Transmitted Deprivation First Report London, 1974, Second Report, 1975 and Third Report, 1977 as well as the literature review in Michael Rutter and Nicola Madge *Cycles of Disadvantage: A Review of Research,* London. Heinemann, 1976.
6. W. G. Runciman *Relative Deprivation and Social Justice,* London: Routledge & Kegan Paul, 1966.
7. Lucy Syson *Poverty in Camden,* London: Institute of Community

Studies, 1975; an earlier study of poverty in Bethnal Green by Lucy Syson and Michael Young reached a similar conclusion though the proportions of immigrants in the Bethnal Green area were very small until recently. See their "Poverty in Bethnal Green" in Michael Young ed. *Poverty Report,* 1974, London: Temple Smith, 1974, pp.100-129.

8. John Greve "The British Community Development Project — Some Interim Comments" *Community Development Journal,* Vol. 8, No. 3, 1973, pp.118-125.

9. National Community Development Project "Inter-Project Report" February, 1974 and the "National Community Development Forward Plan 1975-6", May, 1975.

10. Department of Environment, 1975/76/77.

11. Inner Area Study "Project Report — Lambeth", London, February, 1974, p. 5. Institute of Community Studies *Frustrated Movers: Interim Report,* London, September, 1975.

12. For some idea of these controversies see C. P. Cross "Urban Deprivation and Government Policy with Reference to the Needs of Indigenous and Ethnic Minority People", London, 1974 (unpublished) and N. Deakin "On Some Perils of Imitation" in R.Rose ed. *Lessons from America,* London: Macmillan & Co, 1974, pp. 228-252.

13. Community Relations Commission *Who Minds: A Study of Working Mothers and Childminding in Ethnic Minority Communties,* London, 1975.

14. Working Papers towards an evaluation have been prepared by John Edwards and Richard Batley. These papers are unpublished.

15. A. H. Halsey ed. *Educational Priority: EPA Problems and Policies,* Vol. 1, London: HMSO, 1972 (Vols 2 and 5 were published in 1974).

16. Department of Education and Science "The Educational Needs of Immigrants", White Paper, London: HMSO, 1974.

17. A fuller statement of the work of the Unit can be obtained from their report "A New Strategy for Urban Deprivation", London: Home Office, June, 1974.

18. GLC Policy & Resources Committee "London's Deprived Areas: A Comprehensive Approach", July, 1973 (unpublished).

19. Home Office *Racial Discrimination,* London: HMSO, 1975, Cmnd 6234, para. 13.

20. Department of Environment *Race Relations and Housing: Observations on the Report on Housing of the Select Committee on Race Relations and Immigration,* London: HMSO, 1975, Cmnd 6232, para. 11.

21. Department of Education and Science *Educational Disadvantage and the Educational Needs of Immigrants: Observations on the Report on*

Education of the Select Committee on Race Relations and Immigration,
London: HMSO, 1975, Cmnd 5720, para. 3.

22. Central Policy Review Staff *A Joint Framework for Social Policies,*
London: HMSO, 1975, para. 11.

23. Department of Environment *Census Indicators of Urban Deprivation,*
Working Notes CIUD 6—10 March, 1975; subsequently published in
Sally Holterman "Areas of Urban Deprivation in Great Britain: An
Analysis of 1971 Census Data" *Social Trends,* Vol. 6, No. 5, 1975,
pp. 33-46.

**Chapter 2: Employment Patterns of Ethnic Minority and Indigenous
Communities**

1. David Kohler "Commonwealth Coloured Immigrants and the 1971
Census" *New Community,* Vol. 2, No. 1, 1972-3, pp.80-84; G.C.K. Peach
and S.W.C. Winchester "Birthplace, Ethnicity and the Under-
enumeration of West Indians, Indians and Pakistanis in the Censuses of
1966 and 1971" *New Community,* Vol. 3, No. 4, 1974, pp. 378-393
and G. C. K. Peach "Under-enumeration of West Indians in the
1961 Census" *Sociological Review,* Vol. 14, No. 1, New Series,
1966, pp. 73-80.

2. E.J.B. Rose et al *Colour and Citizenship: A Report on British Race
Relations,* London: Oxford University Press, 1969, pp.179-180.

3. Dennis Brooks *Black Employment in the Black Country: A Study of
Walsall,* London: Runnymede Trust, 1975, p.9.

4. Department of Employment Gazette, Sept. 1975, pp. 868ff.

5. Political and Economic Planning *National Survey of Racial Minorities,*
p. 110.

6. PEP ibid. p. 110 and Table 2 in Appendices.

7. E. J. B. Rose ed. op.cit. pp. 158-159.

8. Ibid. pp. 158-9.

9. E.J.B. Rose, ibid. p. 159.

10. PEP op.cit. p.119.

11. E.J.B. Rose, ibid. pp.173-175.

12. Dennis Brooks op.cit. p.10.

13. CRC *Unemployment and Homelessness: A Report,* London: HMSO 1974.

14. E.J.B. Rose op.cit. p. 181.

15. W. W. Daniel *Racial Discrimination in England,* London: Penguin
Books, 1968 and David Smith *Racial Disadvantage in Employment,*
London: PEP, 1974.

16. Office of Population Censuses and Surveys *The General Household
Survey,* London: HMSO, 1975, Table 4:14, p.178.

17. See for example, D. Kohler *The Employment of Black People in a London
Borough,* London: Community Relations Commission, July, 1974, esp.p.9.

18. Home office *White Paper on Racial Discrimination,* London: HMSO, 1976 Cmnd 6235, p.2.
19. Runnymede Trust Bulletin "Race Relations and Immigration in Britain and the EEC" No. 69, October, 1975.
20. Roger Ballard and Bronwen Holden "The Employment of Coloured Graduates in Britain" *New Community,* Vol. IV, No. 3, 1975, pp. 325-336 and their "Racial Discrimination: No Room at the Top" *New Society,* Vol. 32, No. 654, 1975, pp.133-135; see also W.W. Daniel op.cit. ch. 4 and Neil McIntosh and David smith *The Extent of Racial Discrimination,* London: PEP, 1974 among others.
21. J. H. Taylor "Newcastle Upon Tyne: Asian Pupils Do Better Than Whites" *British Journal of Sociology,* Vol. 54, No. 4, 1973; also Linda Dove's "The Hopes of Immigrant School Children" *New Society,* Vol. 32, No. 653, 1975, pp.63-65 and A. Little "Performance of Children from Ethnic Minority Backgrounds in Primary Schools" *Oxford Review of Education,* Vol. 1, No. 2, 1975, pp.117-135.
22. Roger Jowell and Patricia Prescott-Clark "Racial Discrimination and White-collar Workers in Britain" in S. Abbott ed. *The Prevention of Racial Discrimination in Britain,* London: Oxford University Press, 1971, pp.175-193.
23. Stuart St. P. Slatter *The Employment of Non-English Speaking Workers: What Industry Must Do,* London: Community Relations Commission, 1974; also CRC *The Educational Needs of Children from Ethnic Minority Groups,* London, 1974.
24. PEP *National Survey of Racial Minorities,* op.cit. p. 78.
25. PEP ibid. p. 85. For instance, 44% of Asians finished full-time education at 17 years of age or after compared to 16% of the indigenous population (ibid. p. 84).
26. PEP op.cit. p.117.
27. Dennis Brooks op.cit. p.19.
28. David Smith *Racial Disadvantage in Employment* op.cit. p.84.
29. David Smith ibid. p.88 and Daniel op. cit. p. 210.
30. David Smith ibid. p.88 and Sheila Patterson *Immigrants in Industry,* London: Oxford University Press, 1968, p.193; for some indication of the interest of coloured workers in promotion see D. Kohler op.cit. p. 10, D. Brooks op. cit. p.33 and his *Race and Labour in London Transport,* London: Oxford University Press, 1975, pp.335ff.
31. David Smith op.cit. pp. 86ff.
32. Sheila Patterson *Immigrants in Industry* op.cit. pp.279ff.
33. Department of Employment *Take 7: Race Relations at Work,* London: HMSO, 1972, pp. 6-7.
34. Department of Employment ibid. p.7; also Sheila Patterson *Dark*

Strangers: A Study of West Indians in London, London: Penguin Books, 1965, p.152.

35. Quoted in H. Tajfel and J. Dawson eds. *Disappointed Guests,* London: Oxford University Press, 1965.
36. Sheila Patterson *Dark Strangers* op.cit. p.152; also Daniel op.cit. p.211, Dept. of Employment op.cit. pp.101-2 and Sheila Patterson's *Immigrants in Industry* op.cit. p.194.
37. Dennis Brooks *Race and Labour in London Transport* op.cit. pp.334-5.
38. David Smith op.cit. p.82.
39. Sheila Patterson *Immigrants in Industry* op.cit. p.176 and *Dark Strangers* op.cit. p.153.
40. Sheila Patterson *Immigrants* ibid. pp.177-178.
41. Ibid. p.194.
42. Select Committee on Race Relations and Immigration *The Problems of Coloured School-Leavers,* London: HMSO, 1969, Vol. 1, p.25 among others.
43. E.J.B. Rose et al. op.cit. chap.4.
44. Select Committee ibid. p.13.
45. Daniel op.cit. pp.75-78.
46. David Smith *Racial Disadvantage in Employment* op.cit. p.28.
47. Ballard and Holden op.cit.
50. McIntosh and Smith op.cit. p.26.

Chapter 3: Patterns of Disadvantage in Housing and Housing Allocation

1. For an analysis of these ideologies see M. Harloe, R. Issacharoff & R. Minns *The Organisation of Housing: Public and Private Enterprise in* London: Heinemann, 1974.
2. E.J.B. Rose, et al op.cit. Table 12.2, p.124.
3. OPCS *The General Household Survey* op.cit. Table 2.34, p.77.
4. PEP *National Survey* op.cit. p.53.
5. OPCS op.cit. Table 2, 34, p.77.
6. PEP op. cit. p.152.
7. PEP op. cit. p.160.
8. PEP ibid. p.155 and J. Goodall "The Pakistani Background" in R. Oakley ed *New Backgrounds,* London: Oxford University Press, 1968.
9. PEP op.cit. p. 242; also G. Lomas and E. Monck *The Coloured Population of Great Britain: A Comparative Study of Coloured Households in Four County Boroughs,* London: Runnymede Trust, 1975, pp.25-27 and E. Burney *Housing on Trial: A Study of Immigrants and Local Government,* London: Oxford University Press, 1967, pp. 35-36.
10. OPCS op.cit. Table 2.36, p.78.

11. Rashmi Desai *Indian Immigrants in Britain,* London: Oxford University Press, 1963, p.43.
12. PEP op. cit. p.249, Lomas & Manek op. cit. pp. 27, 36.
13. David Smith & Anne Whalley *Racial Minorities and Public Housing,* London: PEP, 1975.
14. PEP National Survey op.cit. pp. 263-4; also David Smith & Whalley op.cit. and Runnymede Trust *Race and Council Housing,* London, 1975.
15. J. Rex and R. Moore *Race, Community and Conflict,* London: Oxford University Press 1967, p.41 where they describe the pariah status of such landlords and the delicacy of their relationship with local authorities on matters pertaining to public health legislation and its enforcement.
16. Valerie Karn "Property Values Among Indians and Pakistanis in a Yorkshire Town" *Race,* Vol. X, No. 3, 1969, pp.269-284.
17. G. Lomas and E. Monck op.cit. pp.66-72.
18. CRC *Housing Choice and Ethnic Concentration: An Attitude Study,* London, 1977.
19. PEP op.cit, p.240; also Harloe, Issacharoff & Minns op.cit. chaps 2&5 and E. Burney op.cit. p.48.
20. W. W. Daniel *Racial Discrimination* op.cit. Appendix 2.
21. PEP op.cit. p.236.
22. Smith and Whalley op.cit.
23. E. Burney op.cit. pp.39ff; also Stuart Hatch "Constraints on Immigrant Housing Choice: Estate Agents", unpublished report, Bristol University, 1975.
24. PEP op.cit. p.287.
25. PEP ibid. p.245.
26. This is a problem whose potential effect on surveys can be considerable. For a wider discussion of the effect of the racial background of interviewers on interviews, see C. P. Cross "Cultural Factors in Interviewing" in C.P. Cross ed. *Interviewing and Communication in Social Work,* London: Routledge & Kegan Paul, 1974, pp.49-54.

Chapter 4: Policy Issues in Education

1. Gordon Bowker *The Education of Coloured Immigrants,* London: Longmans, 1968, p.8.
2. Bernard Coard *How The Immigrant Child is Made Educationally Subnormal,* London: New Beacon Books, 1971.
3. T. Burgin & P. Edson *Spring Grove: The Education of Immigrant Children* London, Oxford University Press, 1967.
4. H. E. R. Townsend & E. M. Brittan *Organisation in Multi-Racial Schools,* London: NFER, 19 p.1.

5.   For a discussion of some of the philosophical implications of this position during the sixties, see C. P. Cross "Education and Children of Racial Minorities *New Sociology,* Vol. 3, 1976.

6.   A. Little "The Educational Achievement of Ethnic Minority Children in London Schools" in Gajendra Verma and Christopher Bagley eds. *Race and Education Across Cultures,* London: Heinemann, 1975, p.49.

7.   According to this criterion, children were classed as 'immigrants' only if they had lived in England for less than ten years.

8.   Julia McNeal "Education" in S. Abbott ed. op. cit. p.111.

9.   Michael Banton *The Coloured Quarter: Negro Immigrants in an English City,* London: Jonathan Cape, 1955.

10.   Christopher Bagley & Gajendra Verma "Inter-ethnic Attitudes and Behaviour in British Multi-Racial Schools" in Verma & Bagley op.cit. pp.236-262; also Milena Jellinek & Elaine Britain "Multi-Racial Education 1: Inter-Ethnic Friendships" *Educational Research,* Vol. 18. No. 1, 1975, pp.44-53.

11.   Ministry of Education *English for Immigrants,* pamphlet No. 43, 1963.

12.   Second Report of the Commonwealth Immigrants Advisory Council Cmnd 2266, London: HMSO, 1964.

13.   Hansard Vol. 658, cols. 433-4, 27 November, 1963. (My emphasis in italics).

14.   Hansard ibid. (My emphasis in italics).

15.   E.J.B. Rose et al. op.cit. p.269.

16.   A. Little & C. Mabey "Reading Attainment and Social and Ethnic Mix in London Primary Schools" in D. Donnison & D. Eversley eds. *London: Urban Patterns, Problems and Policies,* London: Heinemann, 1973, pp.274-312 esp. Table 9.14 on p.304; also C. Mabey's *Social and Ethnic Mix in school and the Relationship With Attainment of Children Aged 8 and 11,* London: Centre for Environmental Studies, Report No.9, July, 1974.

17.   Nicholas Hawkes *Immigrant Children in British Schools,* London: Pall Mall, 1966, p. 33.

18.   Department of Education and Science *The Continuing Needs of Immigrants, Education Survey No. 14,* London: HMSO, 1972.

19.   L. Dickinson & A. Hobbs et al. *The Immigrant School Learner: A Study of Pakistani Pupils in Glasgow,* London: NFER, 1975.

20.   D. Bainbridge "A Study of the Performance of Pupils of Indo-Pakistani Origins at CSE in a Single Secondary School", unpublished report, Leeds University, 1974; also Little and Mabey in Verma and Bagley op.cit.

21.   J. H. Taylor "Newcastle Upon Tyne: Asian Pupils Do Better Than Whites" *British Journal of Sociology,* Vol. 54, No. 4, 1973, p.11; see

also Bagley's comments on the predominant role given to teacher bias in the selection of samples in the ILEA studies on p.5 of Bagley & Verma op.cit.

22. Sheila Allen & Christopher Smith "Minority Group Experience of the Transition from Education to Work" in P. Brannen ed. *Entering the World of Work: Some Sociological Perspecitives,* London: HMSO, 1975, chap. 5, p.78.
23. Department of Education and science *The Education of Immigrants: Education Survey No. 13,* London: HMSO, 1971, chap. 5.
24. Judith Haynes *Educational Assessment of Immigrant Pupils,* London: NFER, 1971.
25. Ann Dumett *A Portrait of English Racism,* London: Penguin Books, 1973, esp. chap. 4.
26. Margaret Pollak *Todays Three Year Olds in London,* London, Heinemann, 1972.
27. Charles Morrison ed. *Educational Priority: A Scottish Study,* London: HMSO, 1974, chap. 10.
28. Christopher Bagley & B. Coard "Cultural Knowledge and Rejection of Ethnic Identity in West Indian Children in London" in Bagley & Verma op.cit. pp.322-331.
29. David Milner "Prejudice and the Immigrant Child" *New society,* Vol. 22, 1971, pp.556-560.
30. For a survey of some attempts to develop Black Studies in London schools see Raymond Giles *The West Indian Experience in British Schools: Multi-Racial Education and Social Disadvantage in London,* London: Heinemann, 1977.
31. Stanley Coopersmith "Self-Concept, Race and Education" in Bagley & Verma op.cit. pp.144-167.

Chapter 5: Youth Service Provision for Ethnic Minority and Indigenous Youth

1. Quoted in *Immigrants and the Youth Service,* London: HMSO,1969,p.8.
2. Margaret Bone *The Youth Service and Similar Provision for Young People,* London: HMSO, 1972, p.1; this is close to the estimate in *Youth and Community Work in the 70s,* op.cit. p.16.
3. Margaret Bone ibid. p.1.
4. Such as the YMCA Survey in Brixton, the Westhill College Survey "The Coloured Teenager in Birmingham", described in the Hunt Report op.cit. p.42.
5. John Eggleston "A Youth and Community Service for the late 1970s" *Youth in Society,* No. 9, 1975, pp. 7-15; also his *Adolescence and Community: The Youth Service in Britain,* London: Edward Arnold, 1976.
6. Department of Education & Science Youth and Community op.cit. p.82.

Chapter 6: Social Services and Ethnic Minority Communities
1. London Borough of Wandsworth *Statistics of the Social Services Department,* 1974.
2. Peter Boss & J. Homeshaw *Coloured Families and Social Services Departments: A Research Summary,* University of Leicester School of Social Work, 1974.
3. Age Concern. *Elderly Ethnic Minorities,* London, 1974.
4. R. Hood et al. *Children of West Indian Immigrants,* London: Institute of Race Relations, 1970.
5. V. Moody & E. Stroud "One Hundred Mothers" *Maternal and Child Care,* Vol. 111, No. 26, 1967.
6. M. Pollack op.cit.
7. Audrey Hunt *Families and Their Needs,* London: HMSO, 1973,chap.VI.
8. G. Stewart-Prince "Mental Health Problems in Pre-School West Indian Children" *Maternal and Child Care,* Vol. 111, No. 26, 1967.
9. For the results of a major research study of this problem as it affects West Africans in London, see C. P. Cross and C. Ibru "A Portrait of Foster Care: Private Fostering Among Two Generations of Nigerians" *West African Journal of Sociology and Political Science,* Vol. 1, No. 3, 1978, pp.285-305.
10. Gillian Lomas and E. Monck op.cit.
11. Community Relations Commission *One Year On: The Resettlement of Refugees from Uganda in Britain,* London, 1974.
12. C. Jones *Immigration and Social Policy in Britain,* London: Tavistock, 1977.
13. These totals do not tally because each department gave more than one response.

Chapter 7: Conclusions
1. Department of the Environment *Policy for The Inner Cities,* London: HMSO, Cmnd 6845, 1977.

Select Bibliography

Age Concern	*Elderly Ethnic Minorities* London, 1974
Bagley C & B Coard	"Cultural Knowledge and Rejection of Ethnic Identity in West Indian Children in London" in G Verma and C Bagley eds. *Race and Education Across Cultures,* London: Heinemann, 1975, pp 322-331.
— & G Verma	"Inter-Ethnic Attitudes and Behaviour in British Multi-racial schools" in Verma and Bagley op.cit pp 236-262.
Bainbridge	"A Study of the Performance of Pupils of Indo-Pakistani Origins in a Single Secondary School", unpublished report, Leeds University, 1974.
Ballard R & B Holden	"The Employment of Coloured Graduates in Britain" *New Community,* Vol. IV, No. 3, 1975, pp.325-336. "Racial Discrimination: No Room At Top" *New society,* Vol. 32, No. 654, 1975, pp.133-135.
Banton M	*The Coloured Quarter: Negro Immigrants in an English City,* London: Jonathan Cape, 1955.
Bone M	*The Youth Service and Similar Provision for Youth People,* London: HMSO, 1972.
Boss P & J Homeshaw	*Coloured Families and Social Services Departments: Research Summary,* University of Leicester School of Social Work (mineo), 1974.
Bowker G	*The Education of Coloured Immigrants,* London: Longmans, 1968.
Brooks D	*Black Employment in the Black Country: A Study of Walsall,* London: Runnymede Trust, 1975.
—	*Race and Labour in London Transport,* London: Oxford University Press, 1975.
Burgin T & P Edson	*Spring Grove: The Education of Immigrant Children,* London: Oxford University Press, 1967.
Burney E	*Housing on Trial: A Study of Immigrants and*

	Local, London, Oxford University Press, 1967.
Coard B	*How the Immigrant Child is Made Educationally Subnormal,* London: New Beacon Books, 1971.
Coopersmith S	"Self-Concept, Race and Education" in Verma and Bagley op.cit. pp.144-167.
Central Policy Review Staff	*A Joint Framework for Social Policies,* London: HMSO, 1975.
Community Relations Commission	*Who Minds: A Study of Working Mothers and Childminding in Ethnic Minority communities,* London, 1975.
—	*Ethnic Minorities in Britain: Statistical Data,* London, 1974.
—	*The Educational Needs of Children From Ethnic Minority Groups,* London, 1974.
—	*Unemployment and Homelessness: A Report,* London, 1974.
—	*One Year On: A Report on the Resettlement of Refugees From Uganda in Britain,* London, 1974.
Cross C.P.	"Urban Deprivation and Government Policy with Reference to the Needs of Indigenous and Ethnic Minority People" unpublished report, 1974.
— ed.	*Interviewing and Communication in Social Work,* London: Routledge & Kegan Paul, 1974.
—	"Youth Clubs and Coloured Youths" *New Community,* Vol. V, No. 4, 1977, pp. 489-494.
—	"Urban Deprivation and Ethnic Minorities: A Study of The Resource Delivery System in Urban Areas in England" *Human Rights Review,* Vol. 3, 1978 (forthcoming).
— & C. Ibru	"A Portrait of Foster Care: Private Fostering Among Two Generations of Nigerians" *West African Journal of Sociology and Political Science,* Vol. 1, No. 3, 1978, pp.285-305.
Daniel W. W.	*Racial Discrimination in England,* London, Penguin Books, 1968.
Deakin N.	"On Some Perils of Imitation" in R. Rose ed. *Lessons from America,* London: Macmillan, 1974 pp.228-252.
Desai R.	*Indian Immigrants in Britain,* London: Oxford University Press, 1963.
Department of Education and Science	"The Educational Needs of Immigrants", London HMSO, 1974 Cmnd No. 5720.

	The Continuing Needs of Immigrants: Education Survey No. 14 London: HMSO, 1972.
—	*The Education of Immigrants: Educational Survey No. 13,* London: HMSO, 1971.
—	*Immigrants and the Youth Service,* London, HMSO, 1969.
Dept. of the Environment	Race Relations and Housing: Observations on the Report on Housing of the Select Committee on Race Relations and Immigration, London: HMSO, 1975, Cmnd No. 6232.
Dept. of Employment	*Take 7: Race Relations at Work,* London: HMSO, 1972.
Dickinson L. et al	*The Immigrant School Learner: A Study of Pakistani Pupils in Glasgow,* London: NFER, 1975.
Dove L.	"The Hopes of Immigrant School Children" *New Society* Vol. 32, No. 635, 1975, pp.63-65.
Dummett A.	*A Portrait of English Racism*, London: Penguin Books, 1973.
Eggleston J.	"A Youth and Community Service for the Late 1970s" in *Youth and Society,* No. 9, 1975.
Goodall J.	"The Pakistani Background" in R. Oakley ed. *New Backgrounds,* London: Oxford University Press 1968.
Greve J.	"The British Community Development Project — Some Interim Comments" in *Community Development Journal,* Vol. 8, No. 3, 1973, pp.118-125.
Halsey A. H.	*Educational Priority: EPA Problems and Policies,* London: HMSO, 1972.
Harloe M. et al	*The Organisation of Housing: Public and Private Enterprise in London,* London: Heinemann, 1974. Heinemann, 1974.
Hatch Stuart	"Constraints on Immigrant Housing Choice: Estate Agents", unpublished report, Bristol University, 1975.
Holtermann S.	"Areas of Urban Deprivation in Great Britain: An Analysis of 1971 Census Data" *Social Trends,* Vol. 6, No. 5, 1975 pp.33-46.
Hawkes N.	*Immigrant Children in British Schools,* London Pall Mall, 1966.
Hood R. et al.	*Children of West Indian Immigrants*, London: Oxford University Press, 1970.
Home Office	*Racial Discrimination*, London: HMSO, 1975,

	Cmnd No. 6234.
Inner Area Study	*Project Report — Lambeth,* London: 1974.
Institute of Community Studies	*Frustrated Movers: Interim Report,* London 1975.
Jellinek M. & E. Brittan	"Multi-racial Education: Inter-ethnic Friend-ships" *Educational Research*, Vol. 18, No. 1, 1975 pp.44-53.
Jowell R. & P. Prescott-Clarke	"Racial Discrimination and White-Collar Workers in Britain" in S.Abbott ed. *The Prevention of Racial Discrimination in Britain*, London: Oxford University Press, 1971, pp. 175-193.
— & G. Shaheen	*Ethnic Concentration and Housing Choice,* London SCPR, 1974.
Jones C.	*Commonwealth Immigrants and the Statutory Social Services,* unpublished report, University of Manchester, 1974.
Karn V.	"Property Values Among Indians and Pakistanis in a Yorkshire Town" in *Race*, Vol. 10, No.3, 1969, pp. 269-284.
Kohler D.	"Commonwealth Coloured Immigrants and the 1971 census" in *New Community,* Vol. 2, No.1, 1972-3, pp.80-84.
—	*The Employment of Black People in a London Borough* London: Community Relations Commission, 1974.
Little A.	"Performance of Children from Ethnic Minority Backgrounds in Primary Schools" *Oxford Review of Education,* Vol. 1, No. 2, 1975, pp.117-135.
—	"The Educational Achievement of Ethnic Minority Children in London Schools" in G. Verma and C. Bagley eds. op.cit. pp.48-69.
— & C. Mabey	"Reading Attainment and Social and Ethnic Mix In London Primary Schools" in D. Donnison & D. Eversley eds. *Urban Patterns, Problems and Policies,* London: Heinemann, 1973, pp.274-312.
Lomas Graham	*The Inner City,* London: London Council of Social Service, 1974.
Lomas Gillian & E. Monck	*The Coloured Population of Great Britain: A Comparative Study of Coloured Households in County Boroughs,* London: Runnymede Trust, 1975.

McNeal J.	"Education" in S. Abbott ed. op.cit.
McIntosh N. & D. Smith	*The Extent of Racial Discrimination*, London: PEP, 1974.
Milner D.	"Prejudice and the Immigrant Child" *New Society,* Vol. 22, 1971, pp.556-560.
Ministry of Housing & Local Government	*Council Housing: Purposes, Procedures and Priorities,* London: HMSO, 1969.
Moody & V. & E. Stroud	"One Hundred Mothers" in *Maternal and Child Care* Vol. 3, No. 26, 1967.
Morrison D.	*Educational Priority: A Scottish Study,* London, HMSO, 1974.
National Community Development Project	*Inter-Project Report,* London: 1974.
	Forward Plan 1975-76, London: 1975.
Office of Population Censuses & Surveys	*The General Household Survey, 1972,* London HMSO, 1975.
Patterson S.	*Immigrants in Industry*, London: Oxford University Press, 1968.
—	*Dark Strangers: A Study of West Indians in London,* Penguin Books, 1965.
Peach G. C. K. & S. W. Winchester	"Birthplace, Ethnicity and the Under-enumeration of West Indians, Indians and Pakistanis in the Census of 1966 and 1971" *New Community*, Vol. 3. No. 4, 1974, pp.386-393.
—	"Under-enumeration of West Indians in the 1961 Census" *Sociological Review,* Vol. 14, No. 1. New Series, 1966, pp.73-80.
Pollack M.	*Today's Three Year Olds in London,* London Heinemann, 1972.
Prince S. G.	"Mental Health Problems in Pre-school West Indian Children". in *Maternal and Child Care,* Vol. 111, No. 26, 1967.
Rex J. & R. Moore	*Race, Community and Conflict,* London: Oxford University Press, 1967.
Rose E. J. B. et al.	*Colour and Citizenship: A Report on British Race Relations,* London: Oxford University Press, 1969.
Runciman W. G.	*Relative Deprivation and Social Justice*, London: Routledge & Kegan Paul, 1966.
Runnymede Trust	*Race and Council Housing,* London, 1975.
Slatter S. P.	*The Employment of Non-English Speaking Workers: What Industry Must Do,* London: Community Relations Commission, 1974.

Smith D.	*The Facts of Racial Disadvantage,* London: PEP, 1976.
—	*Racial Disadvantage in Employment,* London PEP, 1974.
— & A. Whalley	*Racial Minorities and Public Housing,* London: PEP, 1975.
Social Science Research Council	*Joint Working Party on Transmitted Deprivation* London, 1975.
Syson Lucy	*Poverty in Camden,* London: Institute of community Studies, 1975.
	"Poverty in Bethnal Green" in M. Young ed. *Poverty Report 1974,* London: Temple Smith, 1974, pp.100-129.
Tajfel H. & J. Dawson eds.	*Disappointed Guests,* London: Oxford University Press, 1965.
Taylor J. H.	"Newcastle Upon Tyne: Asian Pupils Do Better Than Whites" *British Journal of Sociology,* Vol. 54, No. 4, 1973.
Townsend H. E. R. & E. Brittan	*Organisation in Multi-racial Schools,* London: NFER, 1972.

Notes